MW01286477

Complete Guide
To Comprehensive Fibonacci Analysis on FOREX

Viktor Pershikov, MFTA

I dedicate this book to my brilliant and beautiful wife.
Ksyusha, I love you.

Table of Contents

Foreword

In 2012, I became the first Russian analyst to be awarded the "Master of Financial Technical Analysis" degree. This achievement resulted from the years-long research on Fibonacci tools and trading on FOREX with Fibo-levels. Following the publication of my research paper in the IFTA annual journal, I received a lot of responses from traders from different countries. They were all interested in my opinion on how to apply Fibonacci tools in trading and it gave me a strong impetus to write this book.

Another event, which convinced me of the need to write a detailed guidebook on technical analysis with Fibonacci tools, was my presentation at the monthly meeting of the Technical Analysts' Society of South Africa in March 2014. My meeting with TASSA members would be impossible without the kind support of Mr. Victor Hugo, Director of Hugo Capital Ltd and Chairman TASSA, and I am extremely grateful to him for this wonderful opportunity.

I am absolutely positive that advanced, correct views on building Fibonacci tools and their application to analysis and trading would aid traders and technical analysts to improve the efficiency of their transactions and forecasts. As compared with other earlier books on the subject, this comprehensive guide is not restricted to various options for building tools and classical ideas of their application, but also describes tailored methods to conclude transactions upon systemic rules for application of Fibonacci tools.

Communicating with traders and technical analysts from different countries (the USA, South Africa, Indonesia) led me to the conclusion that my primary goal, in the capacity of professional technical analyst, lies in the promotion of Fibonacci methods, with their undisputed efficiency. Over the past years, I traded the FOREX market by applying Fibonacci tools only, and the accuracy and efficiency of Fibo-tools are just amazing.

The Comprehensive Fibonacci analysis (CFA) is the main theme of this book; it represents my personal contribution to analytic research (first presented in 2009) and is currently under active development. The CFA was originally intended for the FOREX trading, but at the time being is also applied to the stock and commodity markets, which speaks positively for its "flexibility". To add to this factor, I generally emphasize the other intrinsic CFA features, such as "systemacity" and "simplicity". These are the three pillars that should underlie every area of modern technical analysis, including the Comprehensive Fibonacci analysis.

At present, the main centers of excellence in technical analysis are located in the United States of America, Europe, and Asia Pacific Region. These are large regions with a huge number of professional analysts and their contribution to the development of technical analysis is invaluable. I believe that with the publication of this book and awarding me the Master of Financial Technical Analysis degree, Russian experts will come out of the shadow and the global technical analysis will be supplemented and expanded by unique and effective methods.

With firm belief in the success of my readers,

Viktor Pershikov, MFTA

Introduction

Can trading on FOREX with just Fibonacci tools be effective and profitable? This book says: Yes!

In modern conditions, when the currency market is very challenging, traders worldwide need precise and highly effective methods and strategies to profit from their transactions. The vast majority of time-honored trading systems were developed for the stock and commodity markets, and traders started applying them over time in the FOREX. Accounting for differences in the pattern of price dynamics and volatility in different financial markets, a trading method proven in the stock or commodity markets may be inadequate to the FOREX. Inherent differences between the foreign exchange and other financial markets give impetus to the creation and application of targeted trading systems and strategies that would fit perfectly to the specifics of FOREX price dynamics. These up-to-date and effective trading methods are discussed in this book.

This book encourages the reader to explore a new area of technical analysis – the Comprehensive Fibonacci analysis. Despite the fact that Fibonacci tools are widely known as such, the technical analysis still lacks specific rules for their construction and application to integrated trading. This book is the first to provide the unified and correct plans of constructing the basic Fibonacci tools. Further, it describes the rules and know-how of systemic trading based on these tools, so that the trader can use any of them to ensure effective and profitable transactions. However, the Comprehensive Fibonacci analysis is not a mere trading tool, but an effective mechanism of technical analysis, too. Using the tools described in this book, the trader can easily identify the direction of future price changes and make transactions relying on the comprehensive analysis.

This book builds upon the research of prominent experts in Fibonacci analysis: Robert Fischer, Joe DiNapoli, Derrick Hobbs, Carolyn Boroden, and many others. Their contribution to the development of technical analysis provided for creating a "Comprehensive Fibonacci analysis", an efficient FOREX tool. I've developed further and supplemented the available information on Fibonacci tools with my own original solutions and I'm happy to share them with the readers.

The most important benefit of this book is the possibility to immediately apply the gained knowledge into practice, specifically:

- Perform a correct construction of Fibonacci tools
- Analyze price changes and conclude on the prospects of further rising or falling prices
- Determine the levels, where to open a buy/sell transaction for a particular currency pair

This book is arranged as a step-by-step guide:

Chapter 1 reviews the available tactics and strategies created with the Fibonacci tools underlying the Comprehensive Fibonacci analysis. Various examples cited in this chapter demonstrate the evolution of approaches to the application of Fibonacci tools, from conventional methods used in the stock and commodity markets to modern tactics and strategies using Fibo ratio on the FOREX market.

Chapter 2 introduces the first and the most important tool of the Comprehensive Fibonacci analysis – Retracement. The chapter describes common rules for constructing Fibonacci retracement, taking into account the properties of the level used in this tool. In order to define the maximum trading options, individual and clustered construction of retracement is demonstrated for various currency pairs.

Chapter 3 discusses simple support/resistance clusters identified with Fibonacci retracement. A concept of "cluster" as the key CFA term is first introduced and different types of clusters are described. This chapter continues description of principles for correct constructing Fibonacci retracement started in Chapter 2.

Chapter 4 is devoted entirely to the original author's trading method based on Fibonacci Retracement – internal patterns (IP). The reader is provided with detailed information about the rules of opening transactions, placing stop-loss and take-profit orders upon the discovered patterns. When armed with the information about the retracement construction rules (Chapter 2), the reader is able to immediately start finding patterns on currency pairs.

Price behavior during the formation of internal retracement patterns is described in **Chapter 5**. The reader is provided with information about the auxiliary methods used in effective IP-based trading, as well as opt-out situations when entering into a transaction that should be suspended, due to the emergence of "risk signal".

Chapter 6 reviews Fibonacci projection, an important tool in the Comprehensive analysis. This chapter describes in detail the properties of Projection levels and specific ways to build this tool on the price chart. Non-standard construction situations are considered and trading with this tool is commented.

Another CFA tool, Fibonacci Extension, is explained in **Chapter 7**. This chapter discusses two types of extension and their applications.

Chapter 8 proceeds with the "cluster" concept and the reader is familiarized with methods for finding "composite support/resistance clusters" and their trading application. "Composite clusters" make the basis of CFA trading and consist of levels of correctly constructed tools (examined in Chapters 2-7).

Chapter 9 introduces the "TOC" pattern, the only pattern under CFA, which is unrelated to Fibonacci tools. After studying these materials, the reader will be able to find this pattern on a price chart and apply it effectively, as part of other trading methods based on the Fibonacci tools and discussed above.

Chapter 10 deals with the last CFA tool, Fibonacci Time Projection. This analytic tool allows the reader to detect the time point when the market can form a short-term or mid-term price extremum that initiates the reversal of price movement. Materials presented in Chapters 2-9 will aid the reader to detect market situations when the need to enter a potentially profitable transaction is indicated not only by the level or area of support/ resistance, but also by the very time moment determined with Fibonacci Time Projection.

The final **Chapter 11** presents nine examples of CFA-based transactions made by me in the process of writing this book. Each purchase or sale transaction is described in detail, so the reader can track the logic of decision-making in entering the market, from finding a trigger cause for opening a transaction, up to placing stop-loss and take-profit orders.

Gradual presentation of materials ensures that the reader is first familiarized with each Fibonacci tool and then proceeds to the comprehensive analysis of the FO-REX market.

Now let's get started!

Chapter 1
Classical ideas in the Fibonacci analysis. Introduction to the CFA

Modern developments in technical analysis are based on methods and research conducted by traders and analysts in the previous years, and the Comprehensive Fibonacci analysis (CFA) presented in this handbook is no exception. It builds upon the most popular ideas and methods of technical analysis and is supported by Fibonacci tools. The detailed list of baseline references, which underlie the CFA, is provided in the concluding section of the book. This chapter will explore the most important literature sources and approaches of different authors that enabled creating the CFA – the best tool for technical analysis in FOREX.

1.1. Fibonacci Retracement & Fibonacci Expansion: Joe DiNapoli

One of the books, which laid the cornerstone of the Comprehensive Fibonacci analysis, was «Trading with DiNapoli Levels» by Joe DiNapoli, published in 1998. This was not the first book on the Fibonacci analysis: Fibo ratios and tools were as well mentioned in earlier publications, such as "Trading by the Book" by Joe Ross, "Intermarket Technical Analysis" by John J. Murphy, "The Day Trader's Manual" by William F. Eng, and many others. However, «Trading with DiNapoli Levels» was one of the first books to describe in detail practical applications of Fibonacci Retracement and Extension. These are essential tools in the Comprehensive Fibonacci analysis that allow identifying of the key levels of support and resistance.

In his book, Joe DiNapoli treats Fibonacci Retracement and Extension as «leading indicators». He offers a simple and effective analytical method based on the following Fibo-ratios:

- 38.2 %[1] and 61.8% - for Retracement
- 61.8%, 100% and 161.8% - for Extension

This setup can be considered classic, while the CFA uses a wider range of Fibo-ratios. More levels were added to this list for a more comprehensive analysis and a correct assessment of today's situation on the currency pairs.

Figures 1 and 2 demonstrate examples of using Fibonacci Retracement and Extension in the EUR/USD and GBP/USD charts.

---

1.   In DiNapoli's book, these levels are presented as Fibonacci ratios: 0.382, 0.618, etc. Here, the levels are expressed in percentages, for the sake of convenience.

Figure 1[2]. Retracement levels: 38.2% and 61.8%, EUR/USD, H4

In Figure 1, we can see Fibonacci Retracement built on the EUR/USD down-trend. The price reached the 38.2% level and reversed. Let us turn to the classical definitions of these levels, as stated in "Trading with DiNapoli Levels":

- *Retracement theory states that you measure the vertical distance of the wave between these two extremes of price, (points A and B) and calculate the .382 retracement of this move. At that point, there will definitely, and without doubt, be resistance (selling) to any up move. Retracement theory does not say that prices must stop there, only that there will be significant resistance to further movement.[3]*

Thus, 38.2% makes a strong resistance level for the price; therefore, decline of the EUR/USD pair from this level was quite predictable.

---

2   Charts were generated with MetaTrader software
3   Joe DiNapoli, «DiNapoli Levels: The Practical Application of Fibonacci Analysis to Investment Markets», 1998, p.136

Figure 2. Fibonacci Extension, GBP/USD, H4

In Figure 2, Fibonacci Extension is built on the GBP/USD uptrend. As can be seen from the chart, the price reached the 61.8% level (COP, Contracted Objective Point), and goes down at the moment. This level acted as resistance. Here's what Joe DiNapoli wrote about the Extension levels:

- *The strength of the market during the AB leg, as well as the lack of strength or depth of the retracements on the BC leg, help us to determine which of the three price objective targets is initially met. OP stands for Objective Point; COP for Contracted Objective Point, since it is the smallest of the three possible objectives; XOP for Expanded Objective Point, since it is the largest. Generally speaking, OP targets are met more often than COP targets, before a significant retracement occurs. XOP targets are least frequently fulfilled.* [4]

Obviously, analytic approaches that involve Fibonacci tools can be used in their classical form (especially, "DiNapoli Levels"), as described by Joe DiNapoli in his book. The set of levels suggested in the book was quite adequate for early applications of Retracement and Extension. However, the need to supplement the CFA tools with new levels appeared over time and thus, the variety of situations to be treated with Retracement and Extension expanded considerably. Apart from the classical approach to determining levels of support and resistance, Retracement and Extension are used in the CFA for other purposes, for example, to identify

4 Joe DiNapoli, «DiNapoli Levels: The Practical Application of Fibonacci Analysis to Investment Markets», Coast Investment Software, Inc., 1998, p.141

patterns during the development of correction, which provide the basis for making transactions.

1.2. Harmonic patterns: Larry Pesavento, Scott M. Carney

Another tool of technical analysis underlying the CFA is represented by harmonic patterns, e.g., "Butterfly", "Crab", "The Gartley", etc. Harmonic patterns, as such, are not included in the Comprehensive Fibonacci analysis, since they refer to another area of technical analysis (the same as the EWA is a separate area of technical analysis, which takes Fibonacci tools). Studying harmonic patterns allowed the development of trading methods within the evolving correction and to implement them in the CFA.

Currently, traders make use of a large number of harmonic patterns. They are best described in two remarkable books: "Fibonacci Ratios with Pattern Recognition" by Larry Pesavento and "Harmonic Trading" by Scott M. Carney, which detail the major harmonic patterns and methods of their trading applications. These two books provided the background information to find regularities in the behavior of the price during the formation of correction.

Figure 3 demonstrates a diagram of the popular "Butterfly" pattern, the classical harmonic pattern. In the FOREX market, we can often find the "Butterfly" on various currency pairs. Figures 4 and 5 demonstrate examples of the "Butterfly" pattern on the AUD/USD and USD/CHF.

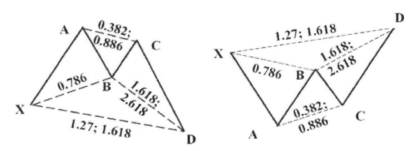

Figure 3. "Butterfly" pattern [5]

---

5. Source: http://www.harmonictrader.com/price_patternsbfly.htm

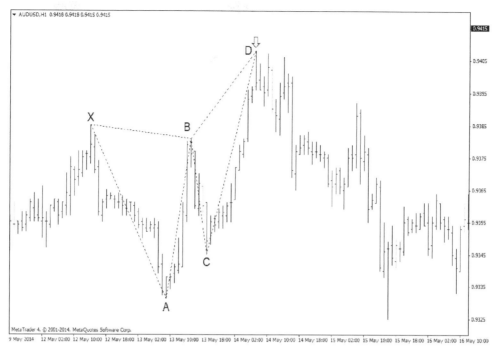

Figure 4. Bearish "Butterfly" pattern, AUD/USD, H1

Figure 5. Bullish "Butterfly" pattern, USD/CHF, H4

An example of another popular harmonic pattern, the "Crab", is shown in Figure 6. The bearish "Crab" pattern was formed on the USD/SEK pair and the price went down thereafter.

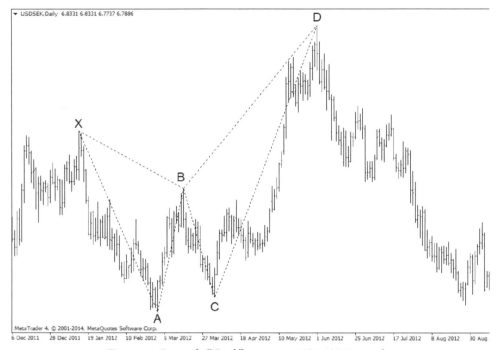

Figure 6. Bearish "Crab" pattern, USD/SEK, Daily

In the above patterns, point D is located outside the X:A trend (at levels 127.2 % or 161.8 %, respectively). Figure 7 demonstrates the pattern, where point D stays within the X:A trend. This pattern is called "Gartley".

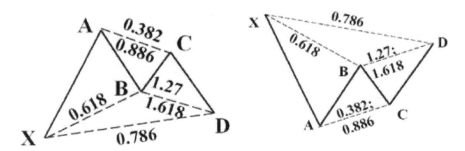

Figure 7. "Gartley" pattern [6]

---

7. Source: http://www.harmonictrader.com/price_patternsgartley.htm

In the case of the "Gartley" pattern, the A:D movement represents the price correction against the X:A trend. This follows from the definition, which states that the correction is a reverse price movement against the current trend.

This pattern was used in studies of the price behavior during the formation and development of correction. The main objective of this research was the creation of trading methods, which would allow entering into transactions in the process of forming harmonic pattern. An example of such trading is a transaction opened at point "C" with the target at point "D", or a transaction opened at point "B" with the target at point "C".

On the one hand, this approach ensures the maximum profits, in case of the correct price movement from point D. On the other hand, if the transaction opened from point D (upon the completed harmonic pattern) is closed with loss, it can be minimized by the earlier gain from trading "inside" the harmonic pattern.

Based on the "Gartley" pattern, a number of typical correction models were developed in the Comprehensive Fibonacci analysis. They are called "internal retracement patterns" and their trading applications will be discussed in Chapter 4.

1.3. Fibonacci time tools: Robert Fischer, Carolyn Boroden

To determine support/resistance levels, the Compreensive Fibonacci analysis includes "time levels" defined with Fibonacci time projections, in addition to Fibonacci tools. The idea of applying Fibonacci time tools was suggested by two books: "Fibonacci Applications and Strategies for Traders" by Robert Fischer and "Fibonacci Trading: How to Master the Time and Price Advantage" by Carolyn Boroden. Both authors made a great contribution to the development of Fibonacci analysis.

In his book (published in 1993), Robert Fischer describes «time goal days» determined with the Fibonacci ratios, as follows:

- *Time goal days are those days in the future upon which a price event will occur. To be able to anticipate a day on which prices will achieve an objective, or reverse direction, would be a step forward in forecasting.* [7]

Here, the key Fibonacci ratios are 0.618 and 1.618. Time levels are constructed between two maximums or two minimums. In this case, we can forecast the day, when the movement of a specific asset will change its direction. Figures 8 and 9 illustrate the application of time levels to determine time goal days.

---

7   Robert Fischer, «Fibonacci Applications and Strategies for Traders», Wiley, 1993, p.104

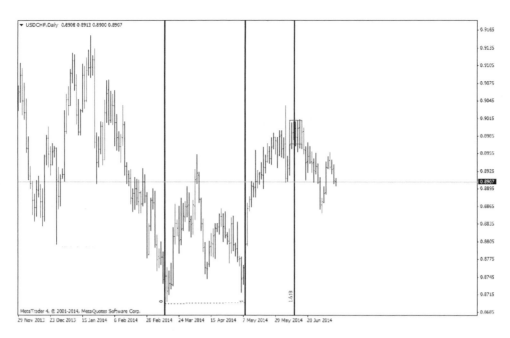

Figure 8. Time goal day determined with Fibonacci time level, USD/CHF, Daily

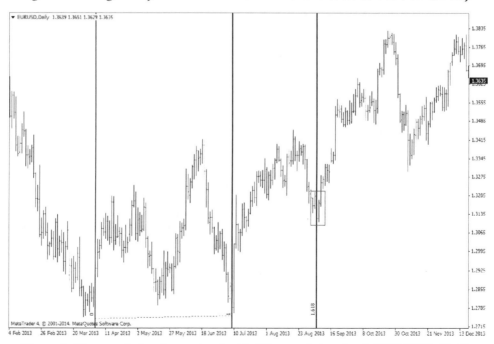

Figure 9. Time goal day determined with Fibonacci time level, EUR/USD, Daily

In her book "Fibonacci Trading: How to Master the Time and Price Advantage", Carolyn Boroden suggested an even more advanced tool: Fibonacci time projection. This tool was equipped with the extended number of levels to be used in trading. The principle of its operation is similar to that of «time goal days»:

- *With Fibonacci time cycle projections, we are looking for a possible trend reversal of whatever the market is doing at the time of the projection(s). For example, if the market were rallying into a .618 time cycle, we would look for a possible high and trend reversal to develop around this cycle, which in this case would suggest that the market would turn back down*[8].

According to the author, the applicable levels of this tool are the following: .382, .50, .618, .786, 1.0, 1.272, 1.618, and 2.618.

An example of Fibonacci time projection is demonstrated in Figure 10. The tool is built on the USD/CAD downtrend. Please note, how accurately we can determine the break-point days with this tool: every time the price passes the next time level, the movement reverses from upward to downward, and vice versa.

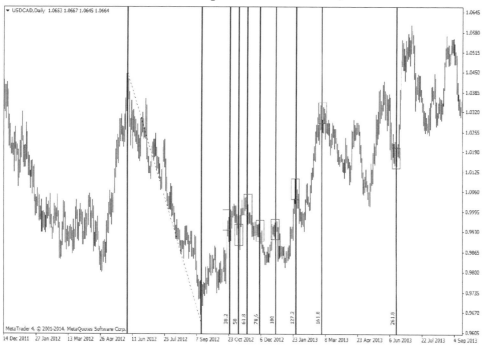

Figure 10. Fibonacci time projection, USD/CAD, Daily

Fibonacci time projection is applied in the CFA in a modified way, rather than in its classical form suggested by Carolyn Boroden. I have developed original meth-

8. Carolyn Boroden, «Fibonacci Trading: How to Master the Time and Price Advantage», McGraw-Hill p. 158

ods to build precisely Fibonacci time projections on historical price movements. To gain the best accuracy, the list of tool's levels was expanded.

The most important advanced features of the Comprehensive Fibonacci analysis include formulation of rules to build time projection on the patterns that precede the rise or fall, instead of arbitrary price movement. With such mode of construction, the efficiency of Fibonacci time projection has increased manyfold. The works of Robert Fischer and Carolyn Boroden, who formulated the basic application principles for Fibonacci time tools, stimulated this development.

1.4. Fibonacci strategies and FibZone: Derrick S. Hobbs

The book «Fibonacci for the Active Trader» by Derrick Hobbs provided an additional starting point for creating the CFA. I consider it the best book ever written on the Fibonacci analysis. The author performed almost a miracle: in addition to the description of specific rules of construction of Fibonacci tools, he outlined applicable, real-life trading strategies based on Fibo-levels.

Derrick Hobbs identified 4 basic Fibonacci tools that can be used in trading and analysis: retracement, expansion, projection, and extension. With these tools, the trader can identify on the chart the areas of possible price reversals, i.e., the so-called "FibZones". By definition, "FibZone" is:

- *Relatively tight ranges of price where a confluence of any combination of at least three Fibonacci price retracements, extensions, projections, or expansions occur*[9].

Once the price has reached such zone, its downward or upward movement may terminate and the price will proceed in the reverse direction (i.e., will go up or down, respectively), as demonstrated by the example in Figure 11.

---

9. Derrick S. Hobbs, «Fibonacci For The Active Trader», TradingMarkets Publishing Group, 1993, p.44

Figure 11. FibZone, GBP/USD, Daily

In Figure 11, FibZone consists of the following levels: 61.8% (retracement X:A), 161.8% (projection A:B:C), and 127.2% (extension X1:A1). Immediately after reaching the resistance area, the price went down and dropped by 900 pips in 16 days.

"Fibonacci for the Active trader" presents a large number of trading strategies; some are the original developments, such as "Heisenberg-200"[10] , "Shark Attack"[11], "Air pockets"[12], etc. Figure 12 demonstrates opening position upon the "Shark Attack" strategy.

---

10. ib., p. 137
11. ib., p. 153
12. ib., p. 165

Figure 12. "Shark attack", USD/ CAD, H4

Despite the fact that Derrick Hobbs's strategies were not included in the Comprehensive Fibonacci analysis, they led to the idea of the systemic trading rules based on Fibonacci tools. These rules eventually made the basis of the Comprehensive analysis, along with time tools and Fib-zones (the so- called "clusters" in the CFA).

In the CFA, clusters represent areas of support/resistance; they are distinguished by the type of tools they are composed of, the degree of their impact on the price; they are also classified into the target or non-target, etc. The CFA clusters evolved from FibZones introduced in "Fibonacci for the Active trader".

The above listed classical trading methods refer to gainful methods. The majority of earlier tools were modified in the CFA, in order to improve the effectiveness of each tool. Expanding the list of levels ensured the larger number of tradable price patterns, while the introduction of specific and unified rules of construction brought forward the integrated approach to Fibonacci-based trading.

1.5. Introduction to the Comprehensive Fibonacci analysis

For a long time, Fibonacci analysis was inextricably linked with the Elliott Wave Analysis. Such tools, as retracement, extension, and time levels, were used to determine the wave structures, wave counting, on financial assets, as well as to predict the levels, where a certain wave (pulse or correctional) can be formed.

Development of the Comprehensive Fibonacci analysis broke the dependence between Fibo tools and the EWA, and now I consider them as two separate, unlinked areas of analysis.

As already mentioned, the Comprehensive Fibonacci analysis rests upon the concepts of Fibonacci tools elaborated in previous years. Here we should emphasize that Fibonacci tools were intended originally for the stock and commodity markets and their application to the FOREX market started only in the last 10-15 years.

The rising popularity of the foreign exchange market, which currently represents a freely available platform for online trading, required a new analytic tool that would satisfy the specifics of its price changes. These specific features include: high volatility, the prevalence of flat movements over the trend ones, and the absence of significant gaps on the charts (FOREX trading runs from Monday to Friday, 24 hours a day). These features make the currency market the most advantageous for Fibonacci-based trading, as compared with other financial markets.

Can we apply CFA tools to other markets, as for example, the stock market? Yes, of course! The principle of construction is the same for all tools of financial markets. However, there are differences, too.

In the FOREX market, the CFA-based trading is guided by the price correction. CFA tools allow us to determine the depth of these corrections and give an opportunity to trade profitably during the development of correction.

In the case, when a trend prevails on some asset of the stock or commodity markets, the CFA-based trading must be reoriented, from trading within corrections to trading in the direction of the emerging trend. This will be possible if the focus is shifted from correction patterns to the area of support/resistance. Entry into the market from these areas will ensure moving in the same direction with the price.

I work in the FOREX market from the very start of my job career as a trader and technical analyst and thus, the book you are holding in your hands, is focused almost entirely on currency pairs and FOREX trading.

I suggested the term "Comprehensive Fibonacci analysis" as early as in the spring of 2009. Over the past 5 years, this analytic area trend was modified significantly, in order to achieve the best trading results with the CFA tools.

What is the CFA in reality? As the name goes, the CFA can aid us in a comprehensive, or integrated, analysis of price movements. The term "comprehensive" implies the following:

- *First, to predict future price movements we use several Fibonacci tools allowing the identification of the key levels of support/resistance;*
- *Second, by using the CFA, the trader analyzes both the levels of support/resistance and the "time" factor: the CFA allows us to determine, where and when*

the price will form a reversal;

- *Third, the CFA is not just a tool for analysis, but also a tool for trading that allows they entry into transactions on the basis of CFA patterns, with account of the predicted price movement.*

Thus, the term "Comprehensive Fibonacci analysis" covers the set of Fibonacci tools and makes us convinced that it is a powerful tool for successful FOREX trading.

The core of the CFA is composed of the following tools:

- Fibonacci Retracement
- Fibonacci Projection
- Fibonacci Extension of types I and II
- Fibonacci time projection

These Fibonacci tools allow us to determine the decision levels – for opening or closing the transaction. In addition to the above listed Fibo-tools, the CFA includes supplementary technical signals to perform transactions.

The vast majority of books on Fibonacci tools mention that, apart from Fibo-levels, the trader must rely on additional signals in his transactions, such as indicators, particular candlestick patterns, etc. The CFA treats this issue as follows: the Fibonacci tools are all sufficient and effective; therefore, other confirmations for opening a transaction are not required. Indicators, candlestick analysis, and volumes are not needed and thus, not included in the CFA: both the level of entry into the market, and the levels of stop-loss and take-profit are determined with Fibonacci tools. No filters or additional signals are needed.

Let me reiterate and emphasize this statement: Fibonacci tools, if they are properly built and applied, need no other confirmations. Now, once I have developed the Comprehensive Fibonacci analysis, traders and analysts shall only use Fibonacci tools properly in their operations. The unified rules of building tools, as well as specific principles of CFA-based trading – all these topics are covered in this book.

To conclude with the introductory review, I want to highlight the fact that up to present, the Fibonacci analysis was under the EWA and did not receive proper development. Now it is an independent tool for technical analysis, which gains popularity and develops from the extensive research of new traders and analysts who take it on board.

And now, let us proceed to studying the Comprehensive Fibonacci analysis.

SECTION I.
Novel ideas in the analysis of corrections

Chapter 2.
Fibonacci retracement and rules for its construction

2.1. Retracement levels

The first CFA tool to be reviewed in this book is retracement. Traders on the stock, commodity, and currency markets use this tool; it is applied both as an independent trading tool, and as a complement to various trading strategies. Quite often, Fibonacci retracement is used as an analytic tool to forecast price changes. Moreover, the price behavior during development of a trend or correction, and its evaluation by retracement allows defining, where the financial asset will move, and how to make a profit from this movement.

According to the classical definition of Fibonacci retracement, this tool is applied in cases when the depth of the correction to the financial asset is evaluated. Since the Fibonacci retracement levels act as support and resistance, the classical definition of retracement implies that correction may end when the price reaches one of the key retracement levels and the price will go on with the trend.

The classic levels are:

- 38.2%
- 50.0%
- 61.8%

In cases when the price correction reaches one of these levels, the correction can be considered complete and we must open transactions in the direction of the previously formed trend.

When we look deeper into this method of using retracement, we are faced with two important questions that must be answered before buying or selling an asset:

1. How to determine during the process of correction, what retracement level – 38.2%, 50%, or 61.8% - will become a key level?

2. What is the probability of the price reversal and its subsequent trend wise movement after reaching one of the key retracement levels?

To answer these questions, the trader needs to create a certain filter, which should be used when opening transactions from the key retracement levels. Such filter excludes the situations when the price, upon reaching key levels, eventually breaks

61.8 % and goes further under the new trend.

Supplementary analytic methods inevitably complicate trading approaches. In the Comprehensive Fibonacci analysis, retracement is used as an independent tool and, given certain features (to be discussed further), retracement can be successfully applied in trading without any filters.

In FOREX trading, I use the following Fibonacci ratios:

- 9% - the value obtained by subtracting the 14.6% level from 23.6%
- 14.6% - the value obtained by subtracting the 23.6% level from 38.2%
- 23.6% - the value obtained by subtracting the 38.2% level from 61.8%
- 38.2%
- 50%
- 61.8%

I use three more levels, in addition to the three classic retracement levels. The 23.6% level is often applied as a support/resistance level, along with the key levels. The 9% and 14.6% levels are very important to the CFA. They allow for a comprehensive use of the price correction by determining the models to open a buy/sell transaction in the course of the price movement.

According to my experience, the 38.2% level in FOREX cannot be attributed to the key levels. Most often, price correction breaks this level and reaches 50% or 61.8%. Therefore, the 38.2% level can be referred to as a strong but non-key level of 23.6%. Both are important in decision-making, but the end of correction is rarely observed here.

The 9% and 14.6% refer to weak levels of support/resistance and are used in finding price reversals only on the Weekly and Monthly timeframes. However, they are very important when it comes to opening transactions in the early stages of correction. This issue is discussed in Chapter 4.

It should be noted that the 9% and 14.6% ratios are currently unused in the Fibonacci retracement. In the context of the Elliott wave theory, they are mentioned in the book «Harmonic Elliott Wave: The Case for Modification of R.N. Elliott's Impulsive Wave Structure» by Ian Copsey. The 14.6% level is also mentioned in «Fibonacci and Gann Applications in Financial Markets» by George MacLean. However, both sources just indicate that these levels can be traded, whereas in the CFA they are not just important, but also effective in retracement-based trading.

Apart from the above listed six retracement levels, other ratios, such as 78.6%, 88.6%, etc., are mentioned in a number of publications on trading and Fibonacci analysis. These levels are important, for example, in harmonic patterns. In my opinion, the above listed six levels are all we need for the Fibo ratios in retracement and no more are required. In this case, the final key level is 61.8%. This level is key not only in terms of its strength, as the level of support and resistance, but also from the point of view that breaking the 61.8 % level indicates a change in the trend direction.

Let's take a look at the schematic plan of constructing retracement:

RETRACEMENTS

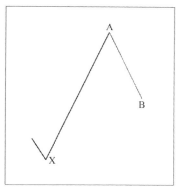 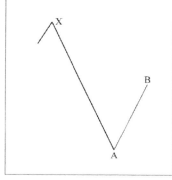

Figure 13. Construction of Fibonacci retracement

Figure 13 shows a schematic representation of two price movements: the (X:A) trend and (A:B) correction in the upward and downward trend. To estimate the depth of the correction and find the important support and resistance levels, we need to build the Fibonacci retracement:

• from the minimum (X) to the maximum (A) in the uptrend, so that the 100% level was included in the minimum (X) and the 0% level – in the maximum (A)

• from the maximum (X) to the minimum (A) in the downtrend, so that the 100% level was included in the maximum (X) and the 0% level – in the minimum (A)

Fibonacci retracement is constructed on the candle shadows (max and min prices). Opening and closing prices are not used in the construction of this tool.

In Figure 13, the segment AB represents the developing price correction. Point B is the current price, both in the ascending and descending correction. Point B should not be located below X in the downward correction and above X – in the ascending correction, otherwise we must rebuild retracement from the segment XA onto the segment AB and further operate with the segment AB, as the new trend, which was previously corrected.

This mode of construction confirms that we have the proper Fibonacci retracement. Currently, traders use different ways to build retracement; however, CFA applies the only correct construction method, as described above: upon the trend, from the minimum to the maximum, or vice versa.

The next figures demonstrate examples of building retracements on the currency pairs USD/SEK, NZD/USD, and USD/CHF.

Figure 14. Fibonacci retracement on the USD/SEK, Daily

The key minimum was formed at point X on the USD/SEK daily chart and after some time, the price reached the local maximum at point A. This was followed by a corrective downturn within the ascending trend. This correction is evaluated with Fibonacci retracement built on the segment XA. Currently, the price reached the 50% level and ascending dynamics is observed on the USD/SEK pair over the last four days.

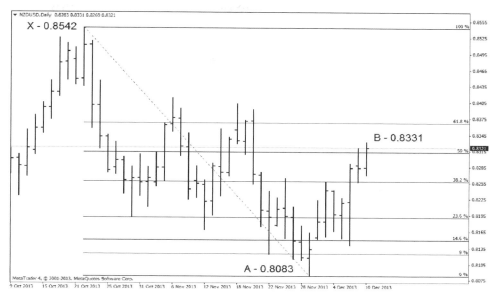

Figure 15. Fibonacci retracement on the NZD/USD, Daily

The key maximum was formed at point X on the NZD/USD daily chart and after some time the price reached the local minimum at point A. Then the corrective uptrend followed. This correction is evaluated by Fibonacci retracement built on the segment X:A. Now the price reached the key resistance level of 50%; therefore, a local downturn of the price from this level could be expected within the descending trend on X:A.

Figure 16. Fibonacci retracement on the USD/CHF, Monthly

Construction of Fibonacci retracement on the long-term downward trend for the USD/CHF pair is demonstrated in Figure 16. The currency pair formed the maximum at point X in July 2001 and, during the next 12 years, it dropped steadily until the minimum at point A was reached. The upward correction evaluated by retracement on the XA segment, has currently reached a strong (though non-key) resistance level at 23.6% and moves downward from this level, in line with the descending trend. Despite the fact that this retracement evaluates the long-term downward trend, its construction provides useful information for the medium and long-term decision making in trading the USD/CHF pair.

When analyzing a certain currency pair, we move between the timeframes and see that trends differ in their lifetime: long-, medium- and short-term trends on financial assets are not equivalent and must be analyzed with different retracements. Moreover, when reviewing several time intervals in the technical analysis, we see the picture of all price changes in its totality, without separating single movements from the whole context.

Therefore, when applying Fibonacci retracement, an important condition is building this tool onto the trends of different duration. Such construction is aimed at defining the length of corrections from different trends, from long-term to short term.

Visual separation of the "price history" on financial assets requires the introduction of special rules for constructing Fibonacci retracement, depending on the duration of price changes within the trend. The basic method of constructing retracement, as mentioned above, is as follows: to build the tool, we need to select the maximum and minimum on the respective trend. Quite often, ambiguous situations occur in the market and in these cases the trader should answer the question: how to select the correct trend for building retracement?

Consistency in building retracement Fibonacci can be achieved in different ways.

One of the common methods is building the retracement in "semi-automatic" mode, where PC-generated indicator shows the trends for the tool, more often – by ZigZag. If we select correct input settings, this indicator will link the important highs and lows of price segments, thus, providing the basis for the construction of Fibonacci retracement. Under this construction method, the main task of the trader is to select the optimal ZigZag's input parameters to cover the price movements as much as possible and, therefore, to evaluate the most corrections from trends of different levels.

The next figure shows an example of constructing retracement on the USD/CAD currency pair, where two ZigZag indicators were set, with parameters «100:0:0» and «60:0:0».

Figure 17. Fibonacci retracements built by ZigZag on the USD/CAD currency pair, Daily

Two Fibonacci retracements were built on the USD/CAD pair (Figure 17) using ZigZag. The indicator with parameters 100:0:0 involves the entire range of the mid-term uptrend marked as X:A. Short-term ZigZag settings (60:0:0) demarcate the final segment of the price upturn marked as X':A within the trend X:A. Thus, Fibonacci retracement on the trend X:A evaluates the prospects of long-term correction, while the retracement on the trend X':A specifies short-term support levels for potential A:B correction (point B is missing at the moment, since the decline from point A is insignificant).

Under such construction, we can view both strong and weak levels of support from two Fibonacci retracements. Our understanding, what level is strong and what is weak, can be used in trading.

In this example, ZigZag parameters (100 and 60) were set with the intention to fit best the situations when Fibonacci retracement is needed quickly and there is no time to analyze trends in more detail.

When applying ZigZag indicator, the borders between the long-term, mid-term, and short-term trends are erased. This is not detrimental to the analysis of historic price changes, because it may be incomplete.

The matter is that when we build retracement upon ZigZag indicator, its parameters play an important role: if we increase or decrease their value, this would lead either to the increase or decrease in the length and number of trends to build Fibonacci retracement. As a consequence, some trends would be lost, because ZigZag fails to show them and, on the contrary, some unimportant price movements would be manifested (especially at low values of ZigZag parameter).

Construction of retracement based on the values of ZigZag indicator is possible. However, building Fibonacci retracement under the CFA is performed upon the other tools, which are equally suitable for all currency pairs on the FOREX market.

2.2. Specifics of the 61.8% level

Before we proceed to the rules of construction retracement in the CFA, let us discuss one of the conditions to be considered by the trader. This condition is related to the selection of correct trend for building retracement, i.e., the specifics of the 61.8% level.

The 61.8% level is the final key level of support/resistance in CFA and the following condition influences construction of the retracement:

• if the price breaks[13] the 61.8% retracement level, then the direction of the trend is changed: the price movement in the former correction becomes a new trend di-

---

13. The breakout of the 61.8% level means fixing the candle body, or 2/3 of the candle body, above or below the key level. If the price pierces the level with shadow of a candle, or one third of 1/3 of its body, this is not considered as a level breakout.

rected opposite to the previous movement.

This feature of the 61.8% level affects considerably the construction of retracement. The strength and importance of this support/resistance level advocates for the following assumption: if 61.8% is broken, retracement must be rebuilt on a new price movement, which transformed from the correction into a new trend.

According to my observations, the vast majority of price corrections on FOREX, which occur above 61.8% of the trend, move further to the 100% level and break it in the capacity of a new trend. This empirical observation leaves no doubt as to the correctness of determining the 61.8% as a key level and the breakout of this level indicates the need to rebuild Fibonacci retracement.

To rebuild retracement from the X:A trend onto A:B correction (the new trend) is quite easy. The figure below illustrates such case.

Figure 18. Breakout of the 61.8% level, retracement built on the X:A trend, EUR/USD, H4

Figure 18 demonstrates the situation when the price breaks the 61.8% retracement level. The place of breakout is indicated by a rectangle. When the price pierced this level, retracement should be rebuilt on the new uptrend that started at point A, and further developed up to the maximum at point B. Accordingly, retracement built on the trend X:A is no longer used in trading. Correct retracement must be built on points A and B.

The breakout of the 61.8% and rebuilding of Fibonacci retracement play a very important role in the process of building retracement on the selected trend. To find the correct maximum or minimum (retracement reference points), we must determine the length of the internal trend corrections. In this case, the 61.8% rule must be considered as follows:

• if the internal trend correction broke the 61.8% level, retracement should be rebuilt. In this situation, we must take the next minimum or maximum, and re-test, whether the 61.8% level is broken by the local correction.

This may seem a bit complicated, but there is nothing difficult in building retracement with due account for the breakout of the key level. All the trader needs is to determine the depth of local trend corrections. If the local correction breaks the 61.8% level, retracement must be rebuilt on the high or low, which satisfies the rule. A diagram showing how to make use of this rule is presented below.

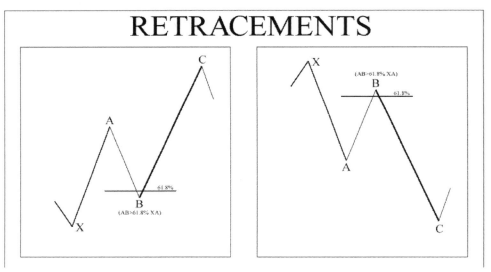

Figure 19. Breakout of the 61.8% level by the local correction, the XA segment

The diagram in Figure 19 demonstrates how to build retracement correctly, subject to the rule of the 61.8% breakout.

Let us assume that a trader wants to build retracement X:C on the upward trend, from the minimum X to the maximum C (left part of the diagram, Figure 19). According to the rule of the Comprehensive Fibonacci analysis, the trader must first estimate the local correction, in terms of penetrating the 61.8% level.

When the retracement is built on the local segment of the X:A trend, we can see that the correction A:B broke the 61.8% level. In this case, point X is not suitable for the construction of Fibonacci retracement, and here retracement should be extended from the "correct" minimum B to the maximum at point C. If we disregard the rule of the 61.8% breakout and build retracement between points X and C, retracement levels would provide the imprecise estimate of correction from point C and trading in such situation would be problematic.

A similar situation is presented in the right part of the diagram, where the local correction from the trend X:A breaks the 61.8% level. Here, building retracement along the entire trend must start from point X, instead of point B, and the retracement must go up to point C.

A couple of examples that demonstrate the principle of retracement construction, with an account for the 61.8% breakout by the local correction, are presented below.

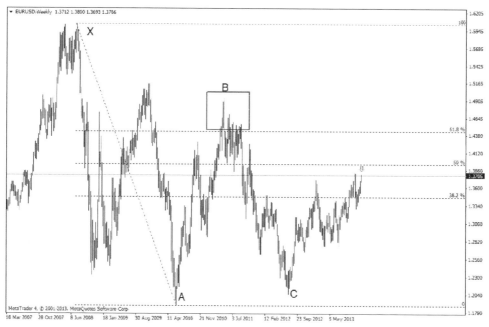

Figure 20. Incorrect construction of retracement on the XA downtrend, EUR/USD, Weekly

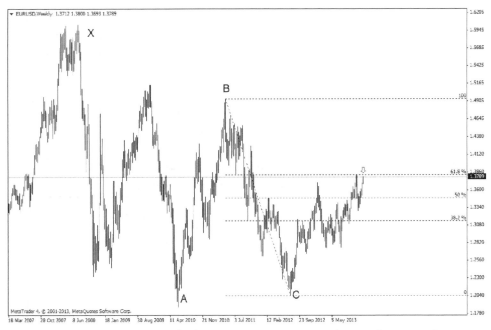

Figure 21. Correct construction of Fibonacci retracement on the XA downtrend, EUR/USD, Weekly

Figure 20 demonstrates an example of incorrect construction of retracement on the X:A downtrend. The local correction A:B broke the 61.8% level (the breakout area is marked by a rectangle). To estimate this upturn from point C, retracement should be built in line with the rules, given the breakout of the 61.8%. The case of correct construction of retracement to evaluate the correctional upward trend is shown in Figure 21, where retracement is built on the BC trend.

It should be noted that this principle of building retracement, with account of the 61.8% breakout, represents an important feature of the Comprehensive Fibonacci analysis and, to be more precise, the main rule of construction, which should not be ignored.

Obviously, this construction method is not the only proper method, since there are numerous rules in the technical analysis that regulate applications of Fibonacci retracement. It is quite possible that in some applications the breakout of the 61.8% level is unimportant. I apply this tool in my operations, because it enhances greatly the efficiency of retracement.

Another example of selection of the point to build retracement, with regard to the rule of the 61.8% breakout, is shown in Figures 22 and 23. This situation illustrates the long-term upward trend on the AUD/USD pair, which occurred in 2001 and formed a maximum at point C.

Figure 22. Breakout of the 61.8% level by the internal correction A:B within the X:C trend, AUD/USD, Monthly

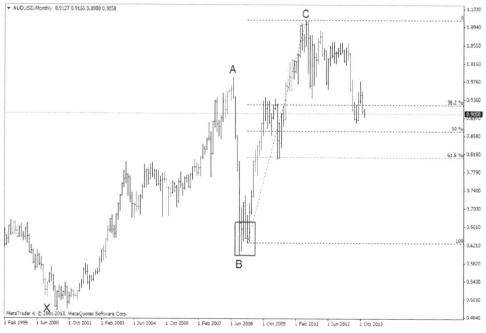

Figure 23. Correct construction of retracement within the upward trend, AUD/USD, Monthly

In Figure 22, points X and C demarcate the long-term upward trend in the AUD/USD pair. The local correction A:B broke the 61.8% level in the first wave X:A within this trend. In this case, the tool cannot be built from point X to point C, according to the rule of the 61.8% breakout. To improve precision of the retracement, the tool should be built in line with the rules and be extended from point B, which ended the local correction of the trend, up to the maximum at point C. Correct construction of retracement on AUD/USD, Monthly timeframe, is shown in Figure 23.

But there is more to come. After selecting point B, as the starting point for constructing retracement, we must ensure that it complies with the rule of the 61.8% breakout by local correction. Figure 23 demonstrates that the retracement at point B is not built on the end of flat, not on the minimum (see Figure 24 for explanations).

Figure 24. Breakout of the 61.8% level by the local correction in point B, AUD/USD, Monthly

In the figure above, point B is zoomed for a more detailed view. It can be seen that if retracement were extended from the minimum X, the local correction A:B would break the 61.8% level from the X:A upturn. Therefore, in this situation point X is unsuitable for starting retracement and the tool should be built from point B (Figure 25).

Figure 25. Correct construction of Fibonacci retracement on the AUD/USD pair, Monthly

The rule of the 61.8% breakout by the local correction is the basic rule, which applies both to rebuilding retracement after the breakout of the key level, and to the principles of building retracement on historical price changes. The above examples illustrate situations when we are forced to select another minimum or maximum to build the retracement under conditions of the 61.8% breakout. This rule is applied in the Comprehensive Fibonacci analysis as the rule of thumb for selecting highs/lows to start building retracement. My experience with this tool confirms that Fibonacci levels, which were generated by constructing retracement on the correct extrema, selected with account for the 61.8% level breakout, are the most effective.

When the trader applies other principles in his Fibonacci-based trading, this important CFA rule may be less important.

The key CFA tool – internal retracement patterns are revealed just in those situations when retracement is built by the rules. The property of the 61.8% breakout directly affects the quality of patterns' identification. The specifics of this key level should not be ignored if the trader wants to get high-quality results with Fibonacci retracement.

We have already mentioned the fact that in order to improve the efficiency of trading with Fibonacci retracement, we need to estimate more than one trend (long-term, mid-term, or short-term). To view the situation in its integrity and use great trading opportunities that appear on different timeframes, retracement should be constructed in a comprehensive manner, with view to estimate the largest possible number of corrections.

2.3. Construction of Fibonacci retracement

The classical division by long-term, mid-term, and short-term trends satisfies most trading situations. Duration of the trend affects the choice of the method to trade financial assets: it may be a long-term retention of transactions, mid-term trade (e.g., swing trading) or short-term trade (e.g., day trading).

As regards building retracement on the financial asset, separation of trends into three types is not always adequate, simply because this classification does not consider their lifetime, i.e., time intervals, which encompass development of this or that trend. Knowledge of the lifetime of a particular trend is needed for finding the trend's extremes within the proper time interval. If the trader had information about the duration of a specific trend, he would only need to select the correct extremes to build retracement.

To simplify the methods of constructing retracement in the CFA and to bring consistency to the construction methodology, trends on the financial assets are divided into five time intervals, according to the number of the main operational timeframes: Monthly, Weekly, Daily, H4, and H1. M5 and M15 timeframes are not applied in the CFA[14].

The following terms are accepted in the CFA: monthly trend, weekly trend, daily trend, four-hour trend, and hourly trend. These designations are used when speaking of the trend defined on the selected timeframe. Naturally, this doesn't mean that, for instance, the monthly trend lies within the terms of one calendar month. The lifetime levels adopted in the Comprehensive Fibonacci analysis are as follows:

- **monthly trend** – 13 years[15] (the starting point of construction is 2001)
- **weekly trend** – 6 years
- **daily trend** – 2 years
- **four-hour trend** – 6 months
- **hourly trend** – two weeks

The starting (reference) point for the monthly trend – the year of 2001 – was taken intentionally. If we review the Monthly charts on various currency pairs, we can see that a steady long-term trend is observed since 2001. Within the main FOREX pairs, this trend represented the stage-wise weakening of the U.S. dollar against its major competitors. After the start of the crisis events in 2007-2008, the weekly trend followed. This is a trend of another type (a strong impact of fundamental data and deflation processes on the price changes).

The daily trend with duration of two years is used in estimating price trends in

14. Fibonacci tools operate on any timeframe with equal efficiency; however, in my operations H4 and Daily are the main CFA timeframes, because they provide the greatest trading opportunities with profit targets at 200-300 pips from a single transaction.
15. As of the time of writing this book (January 2014)

the post-crisis period, which provides greater impact on the current price movements, as compared with the monthly or weekly trends. Running forward, I will note that the price patterns formed on the daily trend are very important in the CFA. At the same time, both the four-trend, which lie within six months, and the hourly trend, which estimates the most recent historical price changes, allow earning on the currency market.

Price changes that occurred prior to 2001 are less relevant in the Comprehensive Fibonacci analysis, because they refer to low-significant price history, both in terms of time and the number of significant events that influenced the dynamics of price changes on the currency market. When we estimate the current price behavior, "ancient" price movements prove to be uninformative. For this reason, we select the year 2001 as a starting point of reference for the analysis of any currency pair.

To build the retracement, we must take the following algorithm:

1. To determine the lifetime of the trend on the timeframe of concern.

2. To find the highest high and the lowest low within the specified time interval.

3. To build Fibonacci retracement, with an account for the rule of the 61.8% breakout.

That's all! It's not that difficult to define correct lifetimes of the trends or to build Fibonacci retracement, but their results will come as a good surprise to anyone who is interested in trading with the Fibonacci retracement.

The rules of construction follow the clear algorithm. Its third section was discussed earlier when we described the specifics of the 61.8% level. We will study the first two sections on the examples of currency pairs, by building a full set of Fibonacci retracements.

The procedure of constructing five Fibonacci retracements on the USD/CHF currency pair is demonstrated below. When several identical tools are built, the color of Fibonacci lines should be varied, to avoid confusion between the tools on different timeframes.

To build the first retracement on the currency pair, we need to open the timeframe Monthly and take the steps of the algorithm: select the period starting from 2001, find the highest high and lowest low within this period, and build the retracement in such a way that the local correction would not break the 61.8% level. The next figure shows construction of the first retracement on the USD/CHF currency pair.

Figure 26. Construction of retracement on the monthly trend, USD/CHF

Figure 26 demonstrates that the USD/CHF currency pair moved downward starting from 2001 till the minimum at point A. The highest price value during this period made 1.8228 (point X), the lowest – 0.7066 (point A). Retracement was built between these points, from the maximum to the minimum. Local corrections did not break the 61.8% level; therefore, retracement was extended exactly upon the defined extremes. Figure 26 demonstrates that correction from the monthly trend reached the 23.6% level.

Figure 27. Construction of retracement on the weekly trend, USD/CHF

In Figure 27, retracement was constructed on the weekly trend. Within the se-lected time interval starting from 2007, the minimum (at point A) was determined unambiguously. To find the highest high for the six-year period, several extremes (X', X'', and X) were tested against breaking the 61.8% level by the local correction. Only the maximum X at 1.1730 proved to be appropriate for building retracement, while the others failed to satisfy this condition. Correction from the weekly Fibo-nacci retracement reached the 61.8% level and this level acted as a strong resistance. If the price would have broken this level, retracement should be rebuilt. Currently, this retracement fits the analysis of correction on the USD/CHF weekly timeframe.

Another rule of retracement construction should be mentioned with regards to this example:

• The 61.8% breakout must be tested on the timeframe, which corresponds to the respective trend of this time interval. For instance, if retracement is built on the week-ly trend, breakout of the 61.8% level must be viewed on the weekly timeframe only.

Figure 28. Construction of retracement on the daily trend, USD/CHF

Figure 28 demonstrates construction of retracement on the daily trend, the USD/CHF currency pair. The lowest low since 2011 makes 0.7066 (point X), and the highest high is 0.9972 (point A). Retracement was built between these points, from the minimum to the maximum. Local corrections did not break the 61.8% level; therefore, retracement was built exactly on the defined extremes. Figure 28 demonstrates that correction from the monthly trend reached the 38.2% support level.

Figure 29. Construction of retracement on the four-hour trend, USD/CHF

Construction of retracement on the four-hour trend, within the time interval of six months, is demonstrated in Figure 29. The highest high is 0.9751 (point X), and the lowest low is 0.8838 (point A). Retracement was extended between these points, from the maximum to the minimum. Local corrections did not break through the 61.8% level and, therefore, retracement was extended exactly upon the defined extremes. Up to the moment, correction from point A did not occur. In case the price continues with a downward movement, retracement should be rebuilt in the lower area, since the price value at point A would decline.

Figure 30. Construction of retracement on the hourly trend, USD/CHF, H1

The final retracement was built on the hourly trend (Figure 30). During two trading weeks, the price formed the highest high and the lowest low in points X and A, respectively. Point X is assigned according to the rule of the 61.8% breakout.

Currently, correction on this short-term trend reached the 14.6% level. If the price continues its downward movement, this retracement should be rebuilt. Moreover, the respective time interval of 2 trading weeks should be kept – while the price would further go down, retracement point X would decline, too.

The logic of constructing each of the five retracements can be demonstrated on the example of the USD/CHF currency pair. Each retracement estimates its own correction and thus, makes possible an effective transaction by providing knowledge on the price behavior within corrections.

In the course of price changes on the currency pair, we sometimes observe situations, when construction is not straightforward and for some reason does not fit the algorithm. Most often, this is explained by the fact that retracement cannot be built, because its trend does not match with the time interval specified for the respective timeframe.

Let's take a look at construction of retracement on the GPB/USD currency pair.

Figure 31. Construction of retracement on the GBP/USD pair, Monthly

Figure 31 demonstrates construction of retracement on the GBP/USD pair. Any retracement starts from the Monthly timeframe. The GBP/USD extreme points were identified for the 13-year period: the maximum X and the minimum A. When building retracement on these extremes, it turns out that the lifetime of the first retracement on the Monthly timeframe makes 6 years, which corresponds to the weekly trend, rather than monthly.

What shall we do in this situation? The answer is simple: the GBP/USD retracement cannot be built on the Monthly chart. Consequently, the first retracement for this currency pair will be built on the weekly downtrend, from point X to point A. Retracement on the monthly trend cannot be built, according to the rules, and therefore, it is absent.

Let's go on.

Figure 32. Construction of retracement on the GBP/USD pair, Daily

The next retracement is built on the daily trend within the interval of two years. Figure 32 demonstrates that the maximum X' and the minimum A' are not suitable for building retracement on the downtrend, because of multiple breakouts of the 61.8% level by local corrections. Therefore, here we have the uptrend instead of the downtrend. Retracement is built from the minimum A' to the maximum A.

However, in the situation the constructed retracement does not match the timeframe of the daily trend, as the distance between points A' and A are equal to six months. Therefore, we have the 4-hour trend. Retracement cannot be built, either on the monthly, or on the daily trend.

The final GBP/USD retracement is built on the hourly trend.

Figure 33. Construction of retracement on the hourly trend GBP/USD, H1

Figure 33 demonstrates that the minimum X' and the maximum A' are unsuitable points for constructing retracement on the hourly uptrend, as the 61.8% level is broken by the local correction A':A. Therefore, we have the downward trend, not an upward. Retracement is built from the maximum A' to the minimum A.

The price reached the key resistance level and the GBP/USD would most likely drop from the 61.8% level. In this case, the hourly retracement must be rebuilt: point A would be shifted in the lower area, along the price movement. Naturally, it would be possible only if the 61.8% level is not broken upward.

The above examples demonstrate clearly that often we cannot build all five retracements on each currency pair. Importantly, if we have no suitable options for building retracement – it should not be built. Constructing the tool upon the wrong trends would lead to false results. Since we open future transactions from the retracement levels, this tool must be constructed strictly by the rules.

The CFA traders often ask, whether we need to rebuild retracement, if the price continues to keep moving between the 0% and 61.8% levels but went outside the timeframe (for instance, the price moves along the retracement levels on H4 for more than six months). In this situation, *retracement should not be rebuilt.*

The matter is that the timeframe represents a method to identify the starting point for a certain trend. The main information retrieved from the lifetime of any trend is the understanding of its starting point and the key extremes. When the price moves between the 0% and 61.8% levels, there is no need to rebuild retracement.

Why delete something that works? The price itself will tell us, when to rebuild the tool. As long as Fibonacci retracement levels aid in concluding transactions – there is no need to rebuild retracement.

Being the CFA author, I build retracements in "automatic mode": I don't need to run all steps of the algorithm, because my experience allows me to accurately select the extremes for building retracement. For the beginners, the algorithm of constructing retracement on a particular trend will be very helpful.

The current templates of retracement for the FOREX market are released weekly at http://fibomaster.com/category/retracement. The ready-made patterns can be used for testing: first, to build one's own retracement and then download the ready template and compare correctness of the construction.

The principle of comprehensive construction of retracement on any trend is an important factor in the analysis of the financial asset. All currency pairs on the FOREX can be appropriately split into trends and the required number of retracements can be built on each trend.

Chapter 3.
Simple support/resistance clusters

3.1. Key and non-key clusters

Clustered building of Fibonacci retracement is applied on the currency market primarily for a search of simple support/resistance areas. In literature sources related to the technical analysis, these price areas are referred to as confluence («K») and Fib-zones. In the CFA, the term "cluster" is used to indicate areas of support and resistance.

• A *cluster* is a price area, where we observe aggregation of Fibonacci levels produced either by clustered building with a single tool, or with a set of Fibonacci tools.

The main difference between the term "cluster" and other terms describing the aggregations of support or resistance levels is that the levels of tools that compose the cluster vary in their strength and significance. For instance, if at a certain price level we observe several weak levels of retracement, it means that this is a weak area of support/resistance and, therefore, it is a cluster of low significance, which should be traded accordingly. If we observe an aggregation of the key Fibonacci levels, from one or several Fibonacci tools, it means that here we have a key cluster of support/resistance – an important tool in CFA-based trading.

Clusters in the CFA are divided into two groups, depending on the number of Fibonacci tools involved in the cluster formation. If a cluster consists of the levels of a single tool (for example, retracement), such cluster is called "simple". When a cluster is composed of the levels of several tools (e.g., Fibonacci retracement and projection, or retracement and extension), this is a "composite" cluster. The significance of Fibonacci levels in the cluster is determined by their attribute as being "key" or "non-key", while the number of levels in a cluster is far less important. For example, a cluster consisting of two key levels is stronger than a cluster consisting of four non-key levels; thus, the quality of the level is a crucial factor.

Under clustered building of retracement on several trends, we operate with simple clusters, i.e., with the areas of support /resistance, where retracements levels from different timeframes are located. A number of examples that demonstrate an importance of simple clusters to trading are presented below.

Figure 34. Daily and four-hour retracements on EUR/GBP, Daily

Figure 34 shows the EUR/GBP currency pair, where two retracements were built on the daily (X1:A1) and four-hour (X2:A2) trends. Under this construction, we can see the resistance cluster and the price approaching it. This cluster consists of two levels: 23.6% daily retracement, and 50% retracement on the four-hour trend. The 50% level is a key resistance level and this price area would undoubtedly act as a resistance cluster. Let's take a look at the chart below.

Figure 35. Key resistance cluster on EUR/GBP, Daily

The cluster of resistance, as identified with two retracements, worked perfectly: Figure 35 shows that the price approached this cluster, but could not break through this strong resistance area and dropped by more than 280 points in seven days. Side note: since the price moved downward, retracement X2: A2 should be rebuilt. Point A2 must be replaced lower, to the updated price minimum.

The downturn of the price from the resistance cluster (Figure 35) is not incidental – it is an outcome of the properly constructed Fibonacci retracement and is due to the fact that the identified resistance cluster was a key one.

Another example of searching for the resistance cluster is shown in Figure 36.

Figure 36. Four-hour and hourly retracements on GBP/USD, Daily

The figure above exemplifies construction of two retracements (four-hour and hourly) on the GBP/USD currency pair. As with the previous example of EUR/GBP, the resistance cluster can be seen in the chart. The next figure demonstrates the price behavior after reaching this cluster. In Figure 37, a closer view of the cluster provides the clearer picture of its constituent levels. To view the cluster components, switch to the minor timeframes.

Figure 37. Four-hour and hourly retracements on GBP/USD, H4

It can be clearly seen that this cluster consists of two levels, 61.8% - from the 1-hour retracement and 9% - from the four-hour retracement. Despite the weakness of the 9% level, it makes a key cluster, because here the 61.8% level is present. Another cluster – 38.2% + 14.6% can be seen in Figure 37. Since these are not key levels, the price pierced it and reached the key cluster.

Figure 38. Key resistance cluster on GBP/USD, H4

On the whole, the weak 9% level should be duly appreciated, as this is a great level for trading and we will discuss it in the next chapter. At the moment, we must perceive the importance of the information provided by the key clusters (Figure 38). The GBP/USD pair reached the resistance area consisting of the levels 9% and 61.8%; after a while, it started downward and the minimum was overwritten. For further analysis, retracement must be rebuilt for a new minimum A2.

Figure 39. Weekly and daily retracements on USD/JPY, Weekly

Another example of application of properly constructed Fibonacci retracements is presented in Figure 39 (take note of the selection of X2 point to build retracement on the daily trend). On the weekly timeframe we can identify a cluster of support consisting of two retracement levels – 38.2% on the weekly retracement and 38.2% on the daily retracement. Despite the fact that the 38.2% levels of both retracements are non-key, they refer to strong levels, as regards the timeframe. In situations, when retracements on senior timeframes enter the game, such support cluster should not be ignored. Upon reaching this cluster, the price completed correction and resumed its upward movement. This situation is shown in more detail in Figure 40.

Figure 40. Support cluster on USD/JPY, Weekly

The strength of the support cluster on the USD/JPY pair was unambiguous (Figure 40): immediately after reaching the cluster, the price started to rise. At the moment, the price overrode the maximum at 0% and the retracement should be rebuilt on a new high A2.

Figure 41. Clusters of resistance on the USD/SEK currency pair, Daily

The final example of application of simple clusters in CFA is demonstrated above. Two retracements were built on the USD/SEK currency pair, on the daily and H4 trends (Figure 41). In the process of correction from A2 minimum, the price approached, in turn, three clusters of resistance. The first represented an aggregation of the 23.6% and 14.6% levels. Since these were weak levels, the cluster kept the price only briefly and after that it moved to the next cluster consisting of levels 23.6% and 38.2%. This was a stronger cluster, as compared with the previous one, and here the price did not just stop, but dropped by more than 200 points. Finally, the price continued development of correction and reached the strongest cluster consisting of levels 61.8 % (four-hour trend) and 38.2% (daily trend).

This is a key resistance cluster. At the same time, downturn of the price from this resistance area was traced in advance, as the key clusters represent places of the price reversal.

3.2. Auxiliary retracement

Construction of several retracements allows the trader to determine price areas, where a cluster of support or resistance is located. A standard method of finding simple clusters implies construction of a retracement, according to the algorithm described above. Situations, when we cannot build all five retracements on a specific currency pair, are quite normal, since the rule of 61.8 % breakout poses restrictions on selection of the point to build a tool. Sometimes we can see situations on the charts, when it deems necessary to build another retracement on the currency pair, which does not match with the number of tools determined earlier for the five main trends. This retracement can play a great role in the case when we are looking for a simple support/resistance cluster. Since its construction does not fit into the algorithm of the main retracements (due to the mismatch in the lifetime of the trend of auxiliary retracement), it can be used only for identifying areas of support and resistance.

The figure below demonstrates the situation on the USD/CHF currency pair; the auxiliary retracement was used to find the resistance cluster.

Figure 42. H4 and H1 retracements on USD/CHF, Daily

Figure 42 demonstrates that retracement built on the X1:A1 trend is obviously insufficient for identifying the resistance cluster on developing correction X2:A2. Here we need an auxiliary retracement, unrelated to any of the five trend retracements. This tool should be constructed by the following rule:

- *To build an auxiliary retracement for finding a support/resistance cluster, we need to find the longest correction within the main trend and build retracement from its end point (maximum or minimum).*

The auxiliary retracement is constructed as follows: first, to find the longest correction (in points) within the main trend, with the already built retracement (any one of the five). After this correction (by timing and, probably, dynamics), a certain new price movement is started and it must be used in construction of the retracement. Figure 40 demonstrates construction of the auxiliary retracement on the USD/CHF:

Figure 43. Auxiliary retracement built on the X2:A2 segment, USD/CHF, Daily

The auxiliary retracement (Figure 43) is constructed from the X2 maximum, which became the end point of internal correction C1:A1. Both tools allowed to define the key resistance cluster, 61.8% + 38.2%.

Figure 44. Price reversal on the key resistance cluster, USD/CHF, Daily

Figure 44 shows that the price reached the resistance cluster and then started downward immediately from this area. Thus, the auxiliary retracement allowed identification of the key resistance cluster.

Figure 45. H4 and H1 retracements on the EUR/USD, H4

Similar to the previous case, retracement built on the X1:A1 trend (Figure 45) does not indicate the resistance cluster to be traded, because X2:A2 retracement estimates the hourly trend. To construct the auxiliary retracement, we need to find the longest correction within the trend X1:A1. To do this, corrections are compared by their size and then the "longest" one is selected.

Figure 46. Internal correction of descending retracement on H4, EUR/USD

In Figure 46, internal trend corrections, suitable for construction of auxiliary retracement, are highlighted. The longest correction is C2 – 165 points, while its neighbors are shorter: 145 and 126 points. Therefore, C2 correction was used to construct the auxiliary retracement.

Figure 47. Auxiliary retracement built on X2:A2 movement, EUR/USD, H4

Following construction of the tool (Figure 47), two key clusters were identified; the price has already reached the first cluster and went downward from it. The breakout of the cluster indicated that the price could reach the final resistance area, which consisted of two levels, 50% and 61.8%. Development of this situation is shown in the next figure.

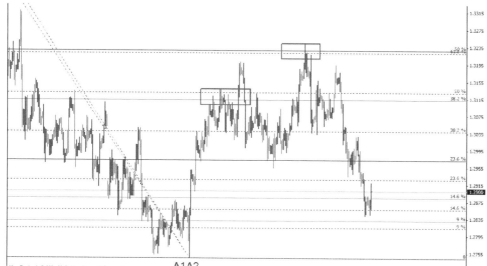

Figure 48. The price reaches the final resistance cluster at levels 50% and 61.8%, EUR/USD-H4

The EUR/USD pair reached successively 2 clusters defined earlier by building the auxiliary retracement. The upper cluster consisted of two key levels and was the strongest. Upon reaching this resistance area, the price reversed immediately and started downward movement (Figure 48).

The price reached two support clusters in succession, as shown in Figure 49. After the deepest correction, the auxiliary retracement was constructed in the trend X1:A1, at the X2 minimum point. Two clusters of support were defined during construction of the auxiliary retracement. These are key clusters; therefore, we could expect that the price would stop on the both. Development of this situation is shown in Figure 50.

Figure 49. Auxiliary retracement X2-A2, USD/CAD, H4

Figure 50. Price reversal on the key support clusters, USD/CAD, H4

Figure 50 shows that the price reached both support clusters in succession and reversed considerably from both zones.

Most often, construction of the auxiliary retracement is needed on the hourly timeframe. If we define clusters of support/resistance on the senior timeframes, the levels obtained from long-term retracements are less important to the H1 timeframe. For instance, weekly retracement is uninformative, if its levels are applied to the H1 timeframe. When the price reverses just on the levels (on the weekly timeframe), the same levels on H1 will demonstrate the flat situation with permanent price breakouts. An example of building the auxiliary retracement on H1 timeframe is demonstrated in Figure 51.

Figure 51. Auxiliary retracement built from the correction end C2, AUD/USD, H1

Figure 51 shows that the auxiliary retracement on AUD/USD was required to find clusters of resistance. It was constructed upon completion of C2 correction, which is the longest internal correction of the hourly trend X1:A1 and actually, it is the only suitable correction for building retracement.

This chart shows the already familiar situation with two clusters, key and non-key. In case the price reached the key cluster, we could expect the start of AUD/USD downward movement in a downtrend. Figure 52 demonstrates how the price behaved in the future.

Figure 52. The price reaches the key resistance cluster and continuation of the downturn, AUD/USD, H1

The price passed the resistance cluster 38.2% + 23.6%, reached the key area, reversed and continued downtrend. Figure 49 shows that the price returned to the resistance cluster again on February 19, thus, giving an opportunity to enter sales for those who failed to sell the asset as soon as the cluster was reached.

A final example of building the auxiliary retracement is shown in Figures 53-54.

Figure 53. Auxiliary retracement on the GBP/USD pair, H1

Figure 54. The price reaches the key cluster and continuation of the downward trend, GBP/USD, H1

The auxiliary retracement (Figures 53 and 54) was constructed after the only internal correction on the GBP/USD hourly trend. The price first reached the non-key and, secondly, the key resistance cluster, which was advantageous for those who planned to sell GBP/USD with the expectations of continued downturn in the descending trend.

Now that we are familiarized with finding simple clusters of support and resistance, we need to understand how to use support/resistance clusters in trade: whether to open the transaction, once the price approached the cluster, or better to wait until the price forms a certain reversal model. We have yet reviewed one type only – simple clusters and further we will discuss another type – composite clusters.

And now it's time to talk about the remarkable graphical models that occur during development of correction and are determined by applying Fibonacci retracement.

Chapter 4.
Internal patterns in Fibonacci retracement and their application in trading

By applying the principles of building a retracement, the trader can easily determine the area of possible price reversal. Relying on this principle, we can form a trading system that would account for the location and strength of clusters on a particular currency pair. However, clusters as such are only indications of places on the chart, where the price can stop. To improve the efficiency of trading on clusters of support and resistance, we need more information about the price in terms, whether it can reverse, or not. If an auxiliary method enables exact determining of the possible price reversal on the cluster, the trader can open a transaction, which would very likely make a profit. To enhance the efficiency of opening transactions on clusters, the CFA offers a unique approach to analysis of the price behavior during development of correction.

Studies of numerous corrections that had occurred in the currency market from 2005 to 2012 revealed that the price followed similar changes while moving between retracement levels. These observations were organized into the trading method and the standard price movements were called "internal patterns of Fibonacci retracement"[16].

  • *Internal pattern of Fibonacci retracement (IP) is the price movement between two retracement levels (Level 1 and Level 2), which suggests the future direction of price movement and levels of placing stop-loss and take-profit orders.*

There are 4 internal patterns in Fibonacci retracement, which are more often formed during development of the correction. Sometimes we can see corrections, where the price does not form internal patterns. The most important for trading are structural corrections, where we can identify patterns for opening transactions to buy or sell a certain currency pair.

Each internal retracement pattern represents the price movement between two Fibonacci levels. Upon completion of this movement, the trader can evaluate the chances of correction development on one of the key retracement levels. Thus, the trader receives information, what level must be used for opening the transaction. Apart from the indication of the entry level, the internal retracement pattern shows the place, where to place take-profit and stop-loss orders.

---

16. Research on the internal retracement patterns is published in the annual IFTA Journal 2014. Link to article: http://ifta.org/public/files/journal/d_ifta_journal_14.pdf, pages 68-79

4.1. The first internal retracement pattern (IP1)

The first internal retracement pattern is the price movement between levels 23.6% and 9%. Schematic plan of this pattern is presented below.

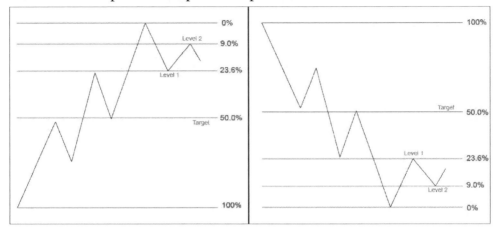

Figure 55. Schematic plan of IP1 pattern

The key levels of the IP1 pattern:
- **L1** = 23.6 %
- **L2** = 9 % (market entry level)
- **Stop** = 0 % (a stop-loss order should be entered at this level. If the price does not break the 0 %, the pattern becomes false).
- **Target** = 50 % (a take-profit order should be placed at this target level).
- **The pattern's P/L ratio** equals 4.6:1

Figure 55 presents a schematic principle of IP1 formation. To form this pattern, the price should touch the 23.6% level and then reach the 9% level. If this movement is formed, correction could be extended up to the 50% level, which would act as a target level in case of opening a transaction from the 9% level. The stop-loss order is placed outside the 0% level.

While forming this pattern, the price can break both the 23.6% and the 9% level. The most important condition is that the 0% level must not be reached, because in this case the pattern is considered false and the price will go on with the trend. In the event that at least one of the key pattern levels (Level 1 and Level 2) is not reached – there is no pattern. The trader can identify a pattern only when the price has reached retracement levels.

These are exhaustive requirements to form the pattern. Just that easy!

And the most amazing thing is that the trader should not bother with finding patterns – we have already constructed five necessary retracements. He must only wait, when the price forms an internal pattern on the constructed retracement.

The figures below demonstrate the principle of IP1 formation.

Figure 56. IP1, USD/CAD, H1

Figure 57. The price reaches the target IP1 level – 50 %, USD/CAD, H1

Figures 56 and 57 demonstrate an example of forming IP1 pattern on USD/CAD. Retracement is built on the hourly trend. First, the price reached the 23.6% level, broke it, and then returned to the 9% level. This is the market entry level with the target – 50%. The sale entry for the stop-loss order is placed slightly above 0%. As can be seen in Figure 57, the price did not reach the stop-loss level and dropped after some time, reaching 50%.

Figure 58. IP1, EUR/USD, H1

Figure 59. The price reaches the target IP1 level – 50 %, EUR/USD

Figures 58 and 59 demonstrate another example of IP1 formation on the EUR/USD currency pair. Here, after reaching the 9% level and opening the transaction to sell, the price was moving between Level 1 and Level 2 for 10 trading days. This did not prevent opening the transaction, as the 0% level was not reached. Ten days later, the price started downward movement and reached the 50% level, thus, ending the IP1 pattern formation.

Let's take a look at a couple of examples of the IP1 pattern.

Figure 60. IP1 formed on the EUR/USD currency pair, H4

Figure 61. IP1 formed on the currency pair USD/SEK, H4

Examples of the IP1 pattern formation on EUR/USD and USD/SEK are demonstrated in Figures 60 and 61. In case of EUR/USD, the price, upon reaching the target 50% level, turned downward sharply. Thus, the price indicated the possibility of ending correction at the target level of the IP1 pattern. In case of USD/SEK, the price oscillated around the 50% level for a while and eventually started upward from this level. At that moment, the transaction to sell from the IP1 had been already closed with profit.

4.2. The second internal retracement pattern (IP2)

The second internal retracement pattern is the price movement between levels 38.2% and 14.6%. Schematic plan of this pattern is presented below.

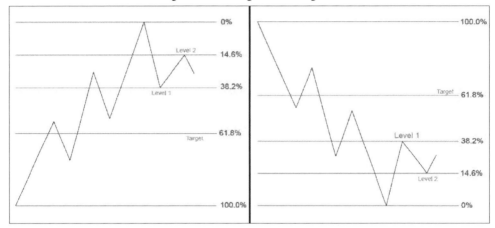

Figure 62. Schematic plan of the IP2 pattern

The key levels of the IP2 pattern:
- **L1** = 38.2 %
- **L2** = 14.6 % (market entry level)
- **Stop** = 0 % (a stop-loss order should be entered at this level. If the price does not break the 0 %, the pattern becomes false).
- **Target** = 61.8 % (a take-profit order should be placed at this target level).
- **The pattern's P/L ratio** equals 3.3:1

The 23.6% level is a strong level of support/resistance, though the price often breaks it, because this level seldom limits correction. In case of breakout at the 23.6% level, we must consider the next retracement level – 38.2%. If the price reaches this level and returns to the 14.6% level, the internal pattern IP2 appears. The target level in this model is the 61.8% level and the level of model cancellation is the same as in the IP1 pattern – 0% level.

When forming this pattern, the price can break through both the 38.2% and

14.6% levels (in IP2, the price often reaches 9%). The most important factor is that the 0% level must not be reached, otherwise the pattern becomes false and the price will go further along the trend. If at least one of the key pattern levels, either Level I or Level II, is not reached – there is no pattern in this case.

The figures below demonstrate the principle of forming IP2 on the FOREX.

Figure 63. IP2, USD/JPY, H4

Figure 64. The price reaches the target IP2 level – 61.8 %, USD/JPY, H4

Figures 63 and 64 demonstrate an example of IP2 pattern formation on USD/JPY. Retracement is built on the four-hour trend: first, the price reaches 38.2% and after that returns to the 14.6% level. This is the level of the market entry, with the target level set at 61%. The stop-loss order to enter sales is placed above the 0% level. As can be seen in Figure 64, the price did not reach the stop-loss level (0%) and after some time started downward movement, reaching eventually the target level.

Figure 65 IP2, EUR/JPY, Daily

Figure 66. The price reaches the target IP2 level - 61.8 %, EUR/JPY, Daily

Figures 65 and 66 present one more example of IP2 formation – for the EUR/JPY currency pair. After reaching the 14.6% level and opening the transaction to sell, the price started moving down to the target level 61.8% and then formed a flat pattern at 50% during 40 days. Trading on senior timeframes, such as Daily, requires some patience. But if the price starts the pattern, we must wait until the target level is reached. Finally, this happened on the EUR/JPY pair and the price reached 61.8%, thus, ending formation of the IP1 pattern.

More examples to illustrate the trading efficiency of the IP2 pattern are given below.

Figure 67. IP2, USD/CHF, H4

Figure 68. End of correction at the 61.8 % level and continuation of the trend on USD/CHF, H4

Figure 67 demonstrates formation of the bearish IP2 pattern on USD/CHF. Following formation of the IP2 pattern, correction eventually reached 61.8%. Figure 68 shows, what happened next to the currency pair. The price completed correction, as the IP2 pattern was formed and the target 61.8% level was reached. Then, the currency pair returned to the ascending trend and continued moving upward, going above the 0% level. Those, who expected the end of correction at the 61.8% level and opened transactions to buy USD/CHF at this support level, could make profit not only from USD/CHF sales on the IP2 pattern.

Figure 69. IP2, NZD/USD, H1

Figure 70. IP2 on GBP/USD, H1

Figures 69 and 70 present examples of IP2 pattern formation with reaching the target 61.8% level on NZD/USD and GBP/USD pairs.

IP1 and IP2 refer to the patterns emerging in the early stages of correction. Understanding of the price direction after formation of IP1 or IP2 provides a great trading opportunity. In IP-based trading, Level 2 indicates the entry into the market with the target level ("Target"). Unlike traditional graphic models, these patterns indicate direction of the price when the pattern is already formed, as well as levels of placing orders and this makes internal retracement patterns a remarkable tool for analysis and trading.

Another not less important factor that confirms IP applicability is the ratio between the potential losses and potential profits. For IP1, this ratio equals to 4.6:1 (potential profit is almost 5 times as much as potential loss!), for IP2 - 3.3:1. Thus, IP1 and IP2 patterns fully comply with the classical rule of money-management, which states that the profit from the proposed transaction must be at least twice as much as the potential loss.

Such features of the IP1 and IP2 patterns leave no doubt that they present an efficient and profitable method of FOREX trading. However, we need to study other patterns that also occur in corrections.

4.3. The third internal retracement pattern (IP3)

Unlike IP1 and IP2, the third internal retracement pattern refers to the patterns of further correction: while IP1 and IP2 appear when the correction just starts forming, the IP3 pattern is formed when the correction has reached the key retracement level – 50%. The following diagram shows formation of the pattern.

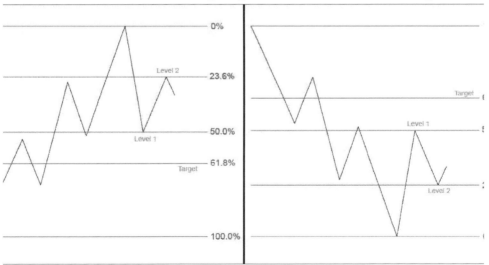

Figure 71. Schematic plan of the IP3 pattern

The key levels of the IP3 pattern:
- **L1** = 50.0 %
- **L2** = 23.6 % (market entry level)

- **Stop** = 0 %
- **Target** = 61.8 % (a take-profit order should be placed at this target level).
- **The pattern's P/L ratio** equals 1.6:1

The most striking feature of the IP3 pattern is the P/L ratio, which equals to 1.6:1. It means that potential profit is by 160% greater than potential loss. This proportion is less than recommended (2:1) and thus, this pattern may seem less efficient than other models with better risk/reward ratio.

However, statistic data on the emergence and implementation of this pattern in the foreign exchange market suggests that its efficiency is high and the suboptimal ratio of potential profit/loss is repaid amply by the great performance of this pattern and the operational frequency of take-profit order. In addition, this pattern has an interesting feature that can improve the P/L ratio (TBD). First, let's see, how this pattern is formed.

While forming IP3, the price must reach the 50% level, reverse, and reach 23.6%. When this movement is formed, we can assume the presence of the IP3 pattern in correction. After reaching the 23.6% level, correction can develop further, up to the 61.8% level, which acts as a target at opening transactions. Stop-loss order in this pattern, as in previous ones, is placed outside the 0% level.

The examples below demonstrate formation of IP3 on the currency pairs.

Figure 72. IP3, USD/CAD, Daily

Figure 73. The price reaches the target IP3 level – 61.8 %, USD/CAD, Daily

An example of IP3 pattern formation on USD/CAD is demonstrated in Figures 72 and 73. Retracement was built on the four-hour trend: the price reached the 50% level and after that dropped to 23.6 %. This is the level of entry into the market with the target level – 61.8%. Stop-loss order at the entry to buy must be placed outside the 0% level. As can be seen in Figure 73, the price did not reach the stop-loss order and after some time started upward, finally reaching the target level.

Figure 74. IP3, NZD/USD, H1

Figure 75. The price reaches the target IP3 level – 61.8 %, NZD/USD, H1

Another example of forming and reaching the target IP3 level is shown in Figures 74 and 75. The pattern was formed on the NZD/USD currency pair. In this situation, the achievement of target 61.8% level was affected by publication of macro-economic data; after that the NZD/USD pair dropped down to the 23.6% level and then surged upward to the target level 61.8%. Macroeconomic publications often act in support of technical situation observed on a particular financial asset. In this case, the trader does not need to decide, whether these data are positive or negative, because trading is based on the technical analysis.

One of the characteristics of the pattern, P/L ratio, was mentioned previously. Another feature is the level of placing the stop-loss order. The distance between levels 23.6% and 0% is large enough, and those, who trade on IP3, may decide that the stop-loss order must be placed closer to the entry point and thus, to reduce this distance. However, I recommend placing the stop-loss just outside the 0% level and here is why (see Figure below).

Figure 76. IP3 pattern on the USD/CHF currency pair, H4

When approaching the 23.6% level, the price often does not stop there and keeps moving to the 14.6% or 9% level (Figure 76). This does not terminate the pattern; however, in such moments the trader is in drawdown and if the price moves to the 0% level, this drawdown can increase. Such situation is normal and rather common. If money-management permits, we can open an additional transaction from 14.6%, with the target level 61.8%. This measure would increase potential profit and if we operate with the IP3 pattern, the drawdown from the 14.6% level will be insignificant. Let's take a look at the figure below.

Figure 77. The price reaches the target 61.8 % level in the IP3 pattern, USD/CHF, H4

Figure 77 shows that the price reached the 9% level, reversed, and made a rapid upturn that ended at 61.8%.

Another example of the same price behavior is demonstrated in Figures 78 and 79.

Figure 78. IP3, EUR/USD, H1

Figure 79. The price reaches the target 61.8 % level in IP3, EUR/USD H1

Once the 23.6% level was reached, the price did not start a reversal under IP3 but moved down to the 14.6% level (Figure 78). This is a common situation with the IP3 pattern. If we already have an open position from the 23.6% level and additional transactions cannot be opened, we just wait when the price reaches the target level. If another transaction can be opened from 14.6% or 9%, it would be appropriate, because this measure would increase potential profit and neutralize the suboptimal profit to loss ratio in the IP3 pattern. Importantly, we must not change placing of stop-loss order: it should be placed outside the 0% level and the transaction should not be closed ahead of time. The fact that the price breaks the 23.6% level and reaches 9% does not mean that the IP3 pattern is not implemented.

4.4. The fourth internal retracement pattern (IP4)

The final, fourth internal retracement pattern represents the price movement between the levels 61.8% and 14.6%. Schematic plan of this pattern is demonstrated below.

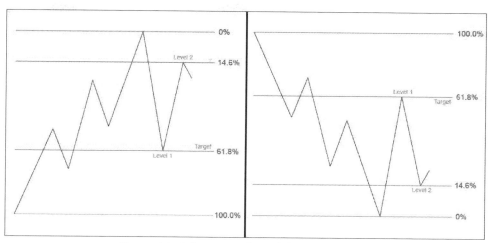

Figure 80. Schematic plan of the IP4 pattern

The key levels of the IP4 pattern:

- **L1** = 61.8 %
- **L2** = 14.6 % (market entry level)
- **Stop** = 0 %
- **Target** = 61.8 % (a take-profit order should be placed at this target level).
- **The pattern's P/L ratio** equals 3.3:1

An important condition in IP4 is that the 61.8% level must not be broken when the price first approaches this level. This rule arises from the rule of breakout of the 61.8 % level, which is used in building retracement. If the price breaks the 61.8 % level, retracement must be rebuilt and, therefore, the IP4 pattern is not formed in this situation.

When the 61% level is reached, the price in correction can reverse to the 14% level. If this happened – we have the IP4 pattern. Its target is retesting the 61.8 % level and further breakout of this support/resistance. The examples below demonstrate formation of the IP4 pattern.

Figure 81. IP4, USD/CAD, Daily

Figure 82. The price reaches the target 61.8 % level in IP4, USD/CAD, Daily

In Figures 81 and 82, formation and performance of the IP4 pattern are shown on the example of USD/CAD. Fibonacci retracement was constructed on the daily trend and during development of correction the price plunged to the 61.8% level, reversed, and started upward, approaching the 14.6% level. Since Level 1 was not broken, we have the IP4 pattern, which indicates that correction will continue and retest 61.8%. The outcome of the pattern formation is shown in Figure 82.

Figure 83. IP4, GBP/USD, Daily

Figure 84. The price reaches the target 61.8 % level in the IP4 pattern, GBP/USD, Daily

Another example of IP4 pattern formation is demonstrated in Figure 83. The pattern was formed on the GBP/USD daily retracement, when the falling price failed to break the 61.8 % level and after that moved upward and reached the 14.6% level. The trader had to identify the IP4 and wait for the further development of correction, up to the 61.8% level. The price behaved itself unambiguously and 61.8% was soon achieved (Figure 84).

The example of forming a short-term IP1 pattern is shown in Figure 85.

Figure 85. IP4, USD/SEK, H1

Figure 86. The price reaches the target 61.8 % level in IP4, USD/SEK, H1

Figures 85 and 86 demonstrate formation of the IP4 pattern on the USD/SEK currency pair. Retracement constructed on the hourly trend allowed defining of formation of the IP4 pattern during the price movement from 61% to 14%. Since the rules of the pattern formation were fulfilled, the proper decision in this situation was opening sales on the currency pair, with the target set at the 61% level. The same as in other internal patterns, the stop-loss order was placed outside the 0% level. Figure 86 demonstrates that the stop-loss level was not reached and the price retested the 61% level.

Internal retracement patterns make an extraordinary, unequalled tool of technical analysis, used to analyze the evolving correction and to trade within this price movement. When applying IPs, the trader gains knowledge about the point of entry into the market and understands clearly, what level of retracement is target in this situation, as well as where to place a stop-loss order.

We don't even need to search for IPs: if retracement patterns are constructed on the chart upon five trends (or less, depending on the situation), we simply wait for the pattern formation. The trader just needs to regularly monitor construction of retracement against changes in the price and rebuild the tool when necessary. The technical picture will change in line with the rebuilding of retracement: new IPs will emerge against new price movements.

In the process of correction, IPs often emerge in groups, rather than individually, which presents a special case in the market. In such situation, the trader can make transactions from different IPs, thus, improving the effectiveness of his trade.

4.5. Sets of internal patterns

Those readers, who have studied carefully the previously presented examples of IPs, may have noticed that other models can also be found in corrections. These are formed earlier or later than the above discussed patterns. So, the reader may already be aware that multiple IPs often occur in correction and they can be used in trading.

Those, who have not yet noticed this remarkable property, are offered to consider the following examples in more detail.

Figure 87. The set of IP1+ IP3+ IP4 on USD/SEK, H1

In addition to the IP4 pattern, two more patterns can be seen in Figure 87. These patterns, IP1 and IP3, were formed during correction. Let's see how this correction developed.

First, the price forms the IP1 pattern with the target 50 % level. USD/SEK declines and reaches 50%, thus, concluding formation of the IP1 pattern. Next, the increase of price up to the 23.6% level indicates that the IP3 pattern is formed, with the target at 61.8%, which is soon reached. Finally, the upturn of the price from 61.8% to 14.6% indicates that the IP4 pattern is formed, with the target at 61.8%, which is also reached without efforts.

Thus, correction on the hourly trend for USD/SEK provided the trader three opportunities to enter the market and make profit on each IP.

Figure 88. The set of IP1+IP2 on USD/CHF, H1

A set of patterns IP1+IP2 (Figure 88) is common in the FOREX market. The USD/CHF sales on IP1 and IP2 were closed successively, with profits exceeding those from trading potentially only one IP.

Figure 89. The set of IP1+IP3 on USD/SEK, H1

Another widespread set of patterns is IP1+ IP3. As demonstrated in Figure 89, the patterns were formed on the USD/SEK (in 2013, this currency pair established a "record" in the number of IP sets). Since the price has not reached the 38.2% level, we are dealing with the IP1 pattern. The IP3 pattern somewhat puzzled those who stood on the buy from 23.6%, as the price dropped almost to the 0% level. When buying USD/SEK on these patterns, I was ready to take losses, if the price would go below 0%. However, the USD/SEK correction reversed in the right direction and, following the rapid upswing, the profit was fixed at the 61.8% level.

Figure 90. The set of IP1+IP2+IP3 on NZD/USD, Daily

Figure 90 presents another challenging set of IPs. Retracement was built on the NZD/USD four-hour trend. Three IPs were identified in the development of correction. Both target levels, 50% and 61.8%, were reached. All three IPs performed perfectly and transactions to buy the NZD/USD pair made a profit.

The final example of a set of patterns is demonstrated in Figure 91.

Figure 91. The set of IP2+IP3 on GBP/USD, H4

The figure above shows an example of a set of patterns IP2+IP3 on the GBP/USD currency pair. Two internal patterns were formed during correction and the price reached the target at 61.8%, thus, increasing profits of those traders who sold the GBP/USD both from 14.6% and 23.6% levels, in line with IP rules.

Trading on sets of patterns improves the effectiveness of trading, because transactions are opened upon several models. Given high effectiveness of internal patterns in FOREX trading, the outcomes of trading upon sets of patterns would be predictably great.

4.6. Meanwhile in stocks

Stock traders often ask me: do internal retracement patterns appear only in the FOREX, or can we find them in the stocks and use in trading or investments?

My answer is straightforward: internal patterns are found not only in the foreign exchange market, but also in the stock and commodity exchange markets. They can be identified on a huge number of financial assets. It does not matter, whether these are Berkshire Hathaway shares or FCOJ futures. Despite the fact that internal patterns were first identified on the FOREX, traders can now apply them to different financial markets. The examples below demonstrate how IPs are formed on the assets of the U.S. stock market.

Figure 92. IP1 on AAPL, Daily [17]

IP1 formation can be traced on the Apple's shares (Figure 92). After a prolonged decline, from 21.09.2012 to 19.04.2013, the share price formed an extremum and reversed. Retracement was constructed on the entire downturn movement (fits into the four-time trend). When developing an upward correction, the share formed the IP1 pattern, started upturn and reached the target pattern level of 50% in five months. AAPL increased by 131.5 USD over this period.

---

17. Charts were generated with Thinkorswim software

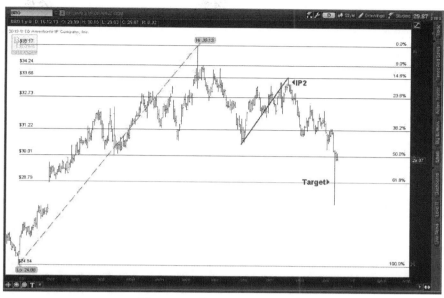

Figure 93. IP2 on BRO, Daily

Figure 93 presents an example of the IP2 pattern on BRO shares. When starting corrective decline from the high of 35.13, security paper formed the IP2 pattern and, once the 14.6% level was reached, went down. Share prices dropped to the 61.8% level in 1.5 months; the drop amounted to 4.87 dollars.

Figure 94. The set of IP1+IP3 on AAMRQ, Daily

As can be seen from the example of IPs on AAMRQ (Figure 94), sets of patterns are found not only on the FOREX. In this example, AAMRQ security first formed the perfect IP1, then reached the 50% level, and IP3 was formed subsequently. The target 61.8% level was reached extraordinarily: the price collapsed down to the target level in one day. This collapse occurred against the information that the U.S. Department of Justice and Attorneys General of six states filed a lawsuit to block the planned merger of American Airlines and the US Airways[18] .

Figure 95. The set of IP1+IP3 on TRLA, Daily

A similar example is presented in Figure 95. Here a set of patterns IP1+IP3 was formed on TRLA.

The situation with IP3 looks particularly intriguing. The price, after relapse to the 50% level, started the next trading day from opening directly at the 23.6% level, declined by 6.16 dollars throughout the trading session and went down further. A few days later, the target 61.8% level was reached.

Figure 96 demonstrates the final example of IP formation on the stock market.

18. For more details see: http://online.wsj.com/news/articles/SB10001424127887324769704579010612415800106

Figure 96. IP2 pattern on / ES (E-mini S&P-500), H4

IP2 pattern was formed on the E-mini S&P-500 (Figure 96). First, the 38.2% level was reached, then the price went to the 14.6% level, and after some time, it reached the 61.8% level. Sales on this pattern yielded 35 points in net profit.

To conclude discussion on the principles of the IP formation and in my capacity as the author of this method, I would like to emphasize that throughout my professional career I have never came across a better trading method than the internal retracement patterns. IP is not a mere trading tool, but rather a new spin in technical analysis. Internal patterns contain really valuable information, which is gradually revealed by traders. Formation of the internal pattern on the financial asset makes a starting point, the beginning of the "great game." From this moment, the trader gets involved in the work and prepares for making precise and efficient transactions based on the CFA.

Behavior of the price during IP formation is also of great importance and needs special discussion.

Chapter 5
Behavior of price in the process of IP shaping

The formed pattern consisting of Fibonacci retracements from different trends simplifies the task of identifying the IP. In this case, you can easily discover internal patterns of various durations (lengths) and select the most appropriate models for your trading. The principles of constructing Fibonacci retracements and assembling internal patterns are reviewed in the previous chapters. Now that we have a chart with forming IP, we can use it in trading by opening transactions, in line with the pattern rules.

However, not every internal pattern reaches the target level. In one situation the pattern works perfectly, whereas in another the price can hit the 0% level earlier than the target level and we make a loss. To select the best patterns out of a large number of models, we need more information about the specifics of IP-based trading.

Let us consider, for example, the first two internal patterns. By now, we have already reviewed the concept of cluster. It represents a very important technical condition for implementing IP1 and IP2 patterns. And even though we discussed simple clusters only, we can conclude that formation of IP1 and IP2 on the support/ resistance cluster represents the most challenging situation, because it provides knowledge about the location, where the price can reverse and the entry point defined upon the IP.

When a pattern appears, the trader should pay attention to the market where this pattern was formed and technical conditions for its implementation, as well as to the behavior of price during formation of the model.

5.1. A pattern in the pattern

The move from Level 1 to Level 2 in the IP is expressed as a short-term trend, where the retracement can be built using the rule of breakdown at the 61.8 % level. Since IPs are formed on different timeframes, the internal retracement pattern can emerge even on a short-term rise or drop of the price within IP. Depending on the situation, retracement on the movement from Level 1 to Level 2 can be either basic (in case it is built upon the pattern), or auxiliary.

The auxiliary IP on the lower timeframe is not used for trading. It indicates that the price is highly probable to hit the target level from the basic IP. Accordingly, the auxiliary IP is used as confirmation of the need to open a "buy" or "sell" transaction at levels of the basic pattern. The examples below show situations when an auxiliary IP was formed on the move from Level 1 to Level 2.

Figure 97. Retracement built on the IP2 pattern, USD/CHF, H4

Figure 98. IP2 pattern, USD/CHF, H1

Figure 97 demonstrates an example of an IP2 pattern, which was formed on the 4-H trend for USD/CHF pair. In the process of the price move from 38.2 % to 14.6 % level, an hourly upward trend was formed and retracement was built on this trend, too (Figure 98). The price formed an IP2 pattern on this retracement, which confirmed the higher IP2. In this situation, the asset should be sold on the basis of two IP2 patterns – the basic and the auxiliary. The auxiliary pattern for hourly time trend should not be used for trading. The pattern highlighted in Figure 98 confirms the overall technical picture. The next figure shows development of this situation.

Figure 99. The price reaches the 61.8 % target level, USD/CHF, H4

Figure 99 demonstrates that the price started its move according to the IP2 rules formed earlier on the 4-H trend. The auxiliary IP2 acted as confirmation of further price decline, down to the 61.8 % target level.

Another example of forming an auxiliary IP is shown in Figures 100 and 101.

Figure 100. Retracement built on the IP1 pattern, USD/SEK, H4

Figure 101. IP3 pattern, USD/SEK, H1

Figure 100 demonstrates the situation with IP1 formation on the USD/SEK currency pair. If an auxiliary retracement is built on price movement from Level 1 to Level 2, we will notice that the price has also formed an internal pattern on this retracement: an IP3 pattern appeared on the auxiliary retracement as an IP1 confirmation (Figure 101). Both patterns suggest that the price would start falling, but in this case IP3 just confirms the need to open USD/SEK sales within a more important pattern, i.e., IP1. Its significance is explained by the fact that this pattern defined the entry point, stop-loss level, and take-profit level. Figure 102 demonstrates how the price behaved after formation of the two IPs.

Figure 102. The price reaches the target 61.8% level, USD/SEK, H4

After formation of the main and auxiliary IPs, the price started moving downward and the USD/SEK has soon reached the target 50% level (Figure 102).

In case of an auxiliary pattern, we are facing a systemic approach to IP-based trading: we have a model for opening a transaction and the model acting as a filter. Thus, when opening a transaction, the trader can build upon those patterns that are confirmed by an auxiliary IP. This would, undoubtedly, enhance the efficiency of trade, but at the same time reduce the total number of patterns to be used in trading and, hence, the total number of entries into the market would not be large.

Let's take a closer look at another example of forming an auxiliary IP. Figure 103 demonstrates an interesting situation, which was formed on the EUR/USD hourly trend.

Figure 103. IP1 and IP2 patterns on EUR/USD, H1

Figure 103 demonstrates an example of a set of patterns (IP1 + IP2) on 1-H retracement for the EUR/USD pair. Internal patterns were formed stepwise and finally they brought the price to 50% and 61.8% levels. We can define, whether auxiliary IPs were present in this situation, by building two retracements on IP1 and IP2 movements.

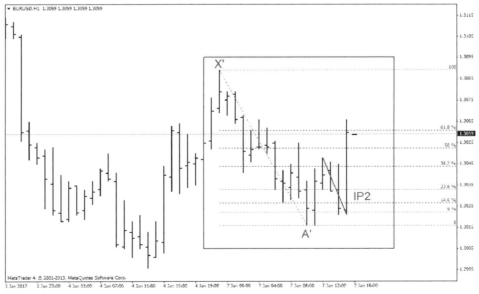

Figure 104. Auxiliary IP2 on EUR/USD, H1

In Figure 104, auxiliary retracement is built on the price movement from 23.6% to 9%. You can see that IP2 is manifested on this retracement, thus, indicating the possibility of price going upward, both upon the short-term pattern and the higher-level model.

Now let's take a look at the movement from 38.2% to 14.6%.

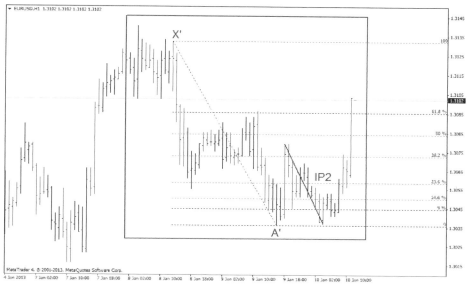

Figure 105. Auxiliary IP2 on EUR/USD, H1

Figure 105 demonstrates that IP2 appeared on the 1-H retracement as an auxiliary pattern, too. Thus, when building retracements on both movements, from Level 1 to Level 2, auxiliary IPs were identified (both – IP2), which indicated the possibility of rising price. Accordingly, price movement to key levels (50% and 61.8%) on 1-H trend retracement was determined not only by the internal patterns of this retracement, but by the auxiliary IPs, as well, which acted as excellent confirmations for opening two transactions to buy the EUR/USD pair.

Construction of auxiliary retracement on the price movement from Level 1 to Level 2 does not disagree with the rules of retracement construction under the Comprehensive Fibonacci analysis. To define simple support/resistance clusters, we use auxiliary retracement and build the tool from the end point of the deepest correction in the trend. Now we have studied another method of constructing auxiliary retracement – price movement from Level 1 to Level 2 in the IP.

It should be noted that internal auxiliary patterns are most often formed in conditions when the main IPs are the first or the second model. However, this method of constructing auxiliary retracement can be applied to any retracement internal pattern.

5.2. The Wolfe Wave in the internal pattern

The first time I came across Wolfe Wave trading was the description in «Street Smarts» book by Linda Raschke and Laurence Connors. At that time I thought this method to be effective and profitable, but since I had already used Fibonacci tools in my work, a standalone application of Wolfe wave was inappropriate for me. However, I realized (and still do) high efficiency of this strategy and modified my views on Comprehensive Fibonacci analysis in a way that Fibonacci tools would be complemented with a Bill Wolfe's model.

Wolfe Wave (Figure 106) is not included as part of Fibonacci analysis and it is used as a supplement whenever needed. I often observe Wolfe waves on various currency pairs. In such situations, I start from the fact that the formed model can aid me in Fibonacci-based trading. My best results were reached when combining Wolfe waves and Fibonacci retracement under conditions when the wave is formed during IP development. In such situations, Wolfe wave can provide a useful aid in opening a transaction upon the IP and can inform pre-emptively when IP implementation is not feasible due to "technical reasons".

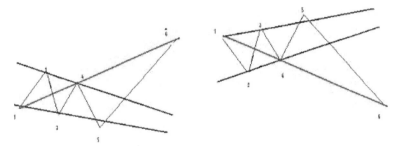

Figure 106. Wolfe Wave [19]

The FOREX assets can form various Wolfe waves differing both in length (duration) and direction (trend-wise or countertrend). Moreover, they are of unequal value to trading, since trading against the main trend prevailing in the market might not always be successful. To save the bother of selecting the priority Wolfe wave, I focus at models that are formed within the IP. Wolfe Wave as part of the IP can be formed either within the movement from L1 level to L2 level, or at the last stage of pattern formation, when the price is at Level 2.

The figure below demonstrates examples of combination of Wolfe waves and IPs. The first example is Wolfe wave and the IP2 pattern on EUR/JPY.

---

19. Source: http://www.investopedia.com/terms/w/wolfewave.asp

Figure 107. IP2 pattern on EUR/JPY, H4

Figure 108. Wolfe wave within IP2, EUR/JPY, H4

Figures 107 and 108 demonstrate this situation by the example of EUR/JPY, where Wolfe wave was formed against forming IP2 pattern on the hourly trend. The bearish Wolfe wave is indicated in Figure 108. You may notice that the price did not stop at point 5 obtained by connecting points 1 and 3. The price almost hit the 0% level, but did not go beyond. With regard to Wolfe wave, the situation did not change, as the price remained within the «sweet zone». After forming a bearish Wolfe Wave within IP2 pattern, the price started downward, first reaching the target point of Wolfe wave, i.e., point 6, and after that – the IP2 target level – 61.8% (Figure 109).

Figure 109. Reaching the target IP2 level, EUR/JPY, H4

When Wolfe wave is formed as an auxiliary indicator, the question arises: what should be considered the target point, either point 6 of Wolfe wave, or Fibonacci target level (50% or 61.8 %)? In such situations, I bear in mind that Wolfe wave within IP is only a supplement that increases the chances of implementing correction to the target retracement level. When opening a transaction upon the IP and Wolfe wave, I set the take-profit level according to the IP schematic plan. As regards Wolfe wave, nothing prevents us to close half of the position at point 6 and thereby capture some profit before the target IP level is hit. This would secure floating profit in case the price starts forming a set of patterns and, for example, IP3 is formed after IP1 or IP2. In any case, the final level to close the transaction profitably is the target Fibonacci level.

An example of Wolfe wave formation within development of IP3 pattern, USD/NOK, is demonstrated below.

Figure 110. IP3 pattern on USD/NOK, Daily

Figure 111. Wolfe wave within the IP3 pattern, USD/NOK, H4

Figure 110 demonstrates an example of an IP3 pattern, which was formed on the USD/NOK pair. This currency pair, same as USD/SEK, refers to exotic FOREX assets, but I regularly use them for trading, since they are very technical and provide lots of opportunities for transactions.

In the process of forming IP3 pattern, the price approached the 23.6% level, where a transaction to sell USD/NOK must be opened, with 61.8% target and a stop-loss order beyond the 0% level. In Figure 111, you can see that upon hitting Level 2, price fluctuation between 23.6 % and 14.6 % formed the Wolfe wave, which indicated that the USD/NOK pair could proceed further correction and Wolfe wave, jointly with IP3 pattern, confirmed the need to keep USD/NOK sales with 61.8 % target level. Development of this situation is shown in Figure 112.

Figure 112. The price reaches the IP3 target level, USD/NOK, Daily

The Wolfe wave that appeared after the price hit the 23.6 % level could be used as an independent pattern, i.e., to enter the sale at point 5 and to close the transaction with profit at point 6. Under the Comprehensive Fibonacci analysis, Wolfe wave acts as an auxiliary element of confirmation and therefore, retaining transactions up to the 61.8% target level would make a more correct solution. Why should we deliberately limit profits when the price is likely to proceed in the same direction as is needed for the transaction?

An example of Wolfe wave formation on the GBP/USD pair is demonstrated below.

Figure 113. IP1 pattern on GBP/USD, H1

Figure 114. Wolfe wave, IP1 and IP2 patterns on GBP/USD, H1

Figure 113 shows how IP1 pattern was formed on the GBP/USD pair and IP2 pattern appeared later, during development of the correction. Thus, we received a set of patterns with two targets – at 50% and 61.8 % levels. Price movements in these patterns made a basis for the bullish Wolfe wave. In this case, Wolfe wave indicates that the price can rise, despite the presence of two IPs. The 50% level falls into the wave's sweet-zone, while the 61.8% level is located far enough from Wolfe wave and is unlikely to be hit. The figure below demonstrates how the price behaved further on.

Figure 115. The price reaches the target IP1 level and continuation of a trend within the bullish Wolfe wave, GBP/USD, H1

Figure 115 demonstrates that the price almost approached the 50% level. This decline is a great opportunity to close the current GBP/USD sales, since the presence of bullish Wolfe wave alerts of the feasible price rise in the future. The GBP/USD pair has not reached the final level of correction – 61.8% and after a drop to 50% the price started upward. Thus, this situation should be treated as follows: to sell an asset within the IP1 (and subsequently, within the IP2), then, after formation of Wolfe wave – to capture profits from GBP/USD sales, from a point of correction start, and to open purchases – aiming to play the formed Wolfe wave with take-profit at point 6. This situation enabled GBP/USD profits, both on the low and on the subsequent high trends.

The final example is shown in Figures 116 and 117.

Figure 116. IP1 on the EUR/USD currency pair, H4

Figure 117. Wolfe wave within the IP1 pattern, EUR/USD, H4

Figures 116 and 117 demonstrate development of Wolfe wave pattern within IP1 pattern on the EUR/USD pair. In this situation, Wolfe pattern was formed far above the target 50% level, so here it was very problematic to decide, what price level should be taken as the sales exit point on IP1. The only sure thing was that, apparently, the target 50% level on IP1pattern would not be hit, because in the first correction stage Wolfe wave was formed as bullish and the price was about to start upward. If the transaction for sale is not closed, the stop-loss order could be triggered.

In this situation, more information about the possibilities of further price rising along the trend would be helpful, with view of buying EUR/USD against the formed IP1. Since the situation is ambiguous, the best option would be closing the sale and waiting for further developments. Some traders could buy EUR/USD on the basis of Wolfe wave. Figure 118 demonstrates how the currency pair behaved after formation of the pattern.

Figure 118. Implementation of Wolfe wave on EUR/USD, H4

After Wolfe wave was formed, the price followed this model immediately and soon reached point 6 of this model by rewriting the 0% level. The IP1 pattern failed due to the obvious reason – appearing an unambiguous bullish technical model during formation of the internal pattern.

Formation of Wolfe wave during the process of price movement from Level 1 to Level 2 is a common situation. Wolfe wave within patterns is not a negative signal; on the contrary, the trader can make transactions based both on IPs, and Wolfe wave. The most important is to understand, how to behave in any particular situation. In one case, Wolfe wave acts as an additional indicator for opening the transaction with a target on the IP, whereas in another – this pattern alerts of possible failure to hit reach the target retracement level after the IP is formed. In the latter situation, the trader can also make money, but the strategy would be based on Wolfe wave, rather than the IP.

5.3. Symmetrical triangles in IP1 and IP2

In the last example of Wolfe wave, I mentioned the issue of cancelling the predicted scenario of IP development to the target level. The Fibonacci trader must perceive the situation when the formed internal pattern could play against him and the market would reach the stop-loss level instead of the expected target.

With regard to internal retracement patterns in the FOREX, the "cancellation scenario" occurs most commonly when a Symmetrical Triangle is formed after forming IP1 or IP2 patterns.

Description of this triangle is given by Jack Schwager in his book «Schwager on Futures. Technical analysis»: a symmetrical triangle is usually followed by a continuation of the trend that preceded it[20].

Symmetrical triangle is often expressed as a model of trend continuation and under the Comprehensive Fibonacci analysis it is particularly useful when formed within IP1 or IP2. If, after entering the transaction from Level 2, the market forms a symmetrical triangle, instead of rising or falling to target levels, you need to close positions at the most acceptable price, because further it would likely move to the 0% level and continue the trend, failing to hit target levels. This prediction is based on long-term observations on the price behavior in IP1 and IP2 against formation of the symmetrical triangle.

Figure 119. Symmetrical triangle in IP1, EUR/USD, H1

---

20. Jack D. Schwager, «Schwager on Futures: Technical Analysis», Wiley, 1995, P.104

Figure 119 demonstrates an example of formation of symmetrical triangle after appearing IP2 pattern on the hourly trend, EUR/USD. According to the pattern rules, sales should be opened at the 14.6% level, but the emergence of a triangle after IP1 formation indicated that the price would unlikely develop a downward move and the level would soon refresh the 0% level.

Figure 120. Continuation of the trend, the price reaches the 0 % level, EUR/USD, H1

Figure 120 demonstrates that the price, after forming a symmetrical triangle, did not move downward within IP2, but instead went high rather quickly and reached the 0% level, thus, canceling the IP2 pattern. Normally, this would trigger a stop-loss order, but losses could be avoided if we consider the presence of a symmetrical triangle and close the transaction to sell at an appropriate time.

Figure 121. Symmetrical triangle in IP1, USD/CAD, H4

Figure 122. Continuation of the trend, the price reaches the 0 % level, USD/CAD, H4

Another example of forming a symmetrical triangle in IP1 is demonstrated in Figures 121 and 122. Here, retracement is built on the time trend (hourly), the USD/CAD pair. The IP1 pattern appeared during formation of upward correction; after that the pair shifted to the flat and subsequently formed a symmetrical triangle. This is a sure sign that IP1 can remain unimplemented, the transaction to buy this currency pair must be closed and more favorable conditions to enter the market should be awaited for. Figure 122 shows that the price in the pattern did not rise above 23.6 %; later, the USD/CAD pair dropped and updated the minimum at 0%.

The last example of a symmetrical pattern is shown in Figures 123 and 124.

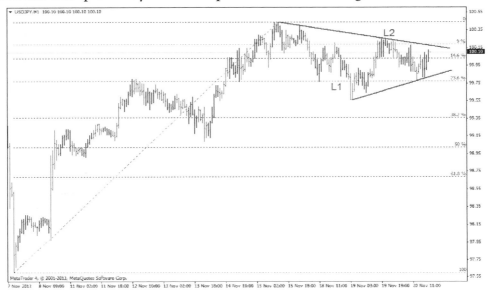

Figure 123. Symmetrical triangle in IP1, USD/JPY, H1

Figure 124. Continuation of the trend, the price reaches the 0 % level, USD/JPY, H1

In the figures above, the symmetrical triangle within IP1 was formed on USD/JPY. Sales were open at the 9% level, according to the pattern. Forming a triangle in IP1 alerted of possible non-implementation of the pattern and possible increase in the price level, with reaching the 0% level and the subsequent refresh of the maximum. The price has soon reversed to an upward trend and cancelled the scenario with reduced price in USD/JPY (Figure 124).

The situation with forming the symmetrical triangle can be viewed from the other side. If the emergence of a triangle indicates that the price can cancel IP and then follow the trend, this feature can be used in trading: open a transaction during formation of the symmetrical triangle. In this case, the 0% level (or even more distant level of prices) stands as a target and (under unfavorable developments) the transaction is closed with losses upon the breakdown from the opposite side of the triangle. This makes one of the trading options based on IP1 and IP2, and here symmetrical triangles are of greatest interest. When a triangle is formed outside IP1 or IP2, it represents a common model of trend continuation, where trading is performed outside the Comprehensive Fibonacci analysis.

In this chapter we reviewed some specifics of price behavior in the process of forming internal retracement patterns. The auxiliary IP and Wolfe wave can emerge during the movement of price from Level 1 to Level 2, which allows defining a model that is highly probable to make profit when reaching target retracement levels. The presence of symmetrical triangles in IP1 and IP2 indicates that the pattern implementation can fail and the transaction at 50% or 61.8% target must be closed without waiting for stop-loss orders.

Once we have examined the behavior of prices in the process of the IP formation, we need to discuss other analytic tools for precise and efficient Fibonacci trading.

Chapter 6
Fibonacci projection: properties of the levels, rules of construction and application in trading

6.1. Projection levels

Another key tool used in the Integrated Fibonacci analysis is a projection (Figure 125).

Along with retracement, Fibonacci projection makes possible determining levels of the end of correction, as well as levels, where the trend can turn to correction.

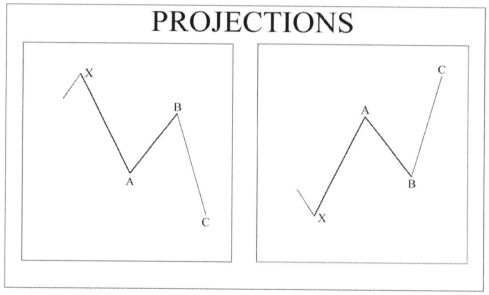

Figure 125. Schematic plan for constructing Fibonacci projection

This tool makes an optimal addition to retracement. Projection is used to define composite clusters and as a stand-alone tool when retracement cannot be constructed and used for the analysis. Relying on the properties of the projection levels, we can identify key support/resistance levels, where the price extremum could be formed.

Figure 125 demonstrates the principle of building Fibonacci projection. This tool is constructed upon two price movements – the first and second wave of the trend, or correction (XA and AB). Construction is started from the point of maximum/minimum price, where the trend or correction (X) was initiated. This method allows for defining support or resistance levels for the future price movement (BC), as well as the important price levels in the correction or trend.

Typically, several levels of Fibonacci projection are used in technical analysis:
- 61.8%
- 100 %
- 161.8%
- 261.8%

Depending on the method of construction, they can act either as support/resistance levels, or as target levels for progressing movement. The most valuable to CFA is the first factor – defining price levels, which represent strong barrier to the price.

Along with the above-mentioned standard levels, I add some more projection levels. Apart from the presence of any level as such, its properties are also important and we should build upon them in our analysis. A complete list of projection levels and their characteristics is provided below.

1. **FE 61.8% (0.618):** *the first level of the tool. It does not act as support or resistance when the price approaches it directly, but on the backward approach, after the breakdown, it transforms into a strong support/resistance level;*

2. **FE 100% (1.0):** *a weak support/resistance level; however, if the second construction wave (AB) is* deep *(greater than or equal to 61.8 % of XA), FE 100% will act as a strong support/resistance level;*

3. **FE 123.6% (1.236):** *a low level of support/resistance, similar to FE 61.8%;*

4. **FE 138.2% (1.382):** *a strong level of support/resistance. It is a key level for direct currency pairs (USD/JPY, USD/CHF, USD/CAD, etc.);*

5. **FE 150% (1.5):** *a strong level of support/resistance; it is a key level for currency pairs containing the Euro component (EUR/USD, EUR/JPY, EUR/GBP, etc.);*

6. **FE 161.8% (1.618) and FE 200% (2.0):** *key support/resistance levels. These levels can end the correction or form the trend extremum.*

The above properties of projection levels are the same for all currency pairs operated at FOREX.

Now we need to specify the definition of a key level. As is obvious, the key level is the strongest level of support or resistance. Price correction can halt at this level. Within a trend, the most important extremes are formed at key levels followed by the price reversal. 138.2% and 150% are key levels to certain FOREX assets. As regards 161.8% and 200%, these levels are the strongest, regardless of the currency pair.

Properties of various projection levels are illustrated by market examples below. A clear understanding of the market performance for a certain level ensures a truly professional approach to trading at the projection levels.

6.1.1. FE 61.8%

The first level is FE 61.8% (Figures 126 and 127). By its specifics, this level gives way to the price when it approaches it for the first time round. But if the price returns back to FE 61.8% after the breakdown, it acts as strong support or resistance. This is a common principle of price behavior in technical analysis when the price retests a certain level after the breakdown, which is particularly noticeable in the case of FE 61.8%.

Figure 126. Fibonacci projection on EUR/USD, H4

Figure 127. Fibonacci projection on GBP/USD, H1

Figure 126 demonstrates how the price broke the FE 61.8% level and reversed back to it again after some time. In this case, FE 61.8% acted as a support level and the price raced up after hitting it. After some time, the situation repeated similarly and the level acted again as a strong support.

The same pattern can be seen in Figure 127. Here the price made a triple attempt to break the FE 61.8% support level, but failed each time and the GBP/USD pair maintained its upward move. FE 61.8% acted as an excellent level of support.

6.1.2. FE 100%

The next level in our list is FE 100%.

Figure 128. Projection on USD/CHF, AB> 61.8% XA, H1

Figure 129. Projection on USD/JPY, AB> 61.8% XA, H4

Figures 128 and 129 demonstrate examples of the price movement at FE 100%. According to its property, when a segment AB is greater than, or equal to, 61.8 % of the segment XA, FE 100% will act as a strong resistance/support level, as observed in Figs. 128 and 129. In both examples, the second projection wave (AB) was greater than 61.8 % of the (XA) wave and the FE 100% level acted both as strong support and strong resistance.

In case, if the AB wave is less than 61.8 % of XA wave, the FE 100% level is unlikely to meet high expectations. An example of such situation is demonstrated in Figure 130.

Figure 130. Projection on USD/CAD, AB <61.8% XA, Daily

Note that correction AB in the figure above has not yet reached the 61.8 % level of XA. In this situation, the FE 100% level fails to act as a price barrier, as can be seen in the chart: when the price reached FE 100%, it failed to push off effectively. In this situation, the level did not act as resistance.

6.1.3. FE 123.6%

The next level of extension – FE 123.6% - is a relatively weak support/resistance level. It is of little value to trading and its operation is similar to that of FE 61.8%: this level acts as support/resistance when triggered by the breakdown and after the price returns back to this level. However, this level can be used for opening transactions under composite clusters and here additional levels of Fibonacci tools balance its weakness.

Figure 131. Projection level FE 123.6%, GBP/USD, Daily

Figure 131 demonstrates an example of the analysis performed for the GBP/USD upward trend with use of FE 123.6%. Projection is built on the first and second uptrend waves (XA:AB) and the level was broken when the price approached FE 123.6%. After some time, the price started downward and approached the FE 123.6% again, but in this case it acted as a support level, according to its properties, and held the price, which continued uptrend thereafter. Similar examples of price behavior at this level can be found in a number of other situations.

6.1.4. FE 138.2%

FE 138.2% represents an important support/resistance level. For the vast majority of financial assets this level acts as strong support or resistance, capable of holding the price. This is the first significant level that can stop the price unconditionally (FE 100 % is strong under certain conditions only). Along with that, for certain FOREX pairs FE 138.2% acts as a key level – i.e., the level, where the price can form a reversal and complete the price movement. These are currency pairs, where USD stands as the first member: USD/JPY, USD/SEK, USD/CAD, USD/CHF, etc. This level is best manifested in these currency pairs, whereas for the others it should be considered only as strong support or resistance upon confirmation.

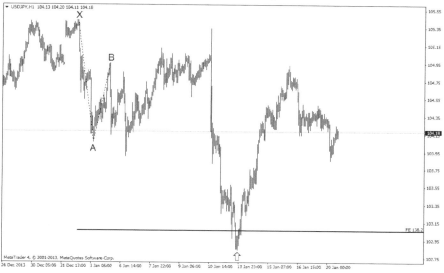

Figure 132. Projection level FE 138.2%, USD/JPY, H1

Figure 133. Projection level FE 138.2%, USD/CAD, H1

Figures 132 and 133 demonstrate examples of FE 138.2% performance as the key level for USD/JPY and USD/CAD currency pairs. Figure 132 shows that the price developed a downward correction and reached support in the form of a key level – FE 138.2%. After a quick drop (completed at key support), an upward move started, which played back almost all price drops. In this case, projection was built on the first and second wave of downward correction - XA:AB.

Figure 133 shows a similar picture. Following a steady rise, the price hit FE 138.2% and sustained a flat at this resistance level for some time. Finally, the price started to decline from FE 138.2%, forming a downward correction during this process.

Take a close look at Figure 133. Do you see here, at FE 138.2%, a standard model that we have already discussed in this book? If the model is not clearly visible, re-examine carefully the chapter on internal patterns of Fibonacci retracement.

Figure 134. Projection level FE 138.2%, NZD/USD, H1

Figure 134 demonstrates an example of constructing the projection on the NZD/USD uptrend. FE 138.2% is not a key level for this pair, and therefore, to enter the sales from this level we must be convinced that the price could actually decline from this resistance. In other words, it is important to understand, whether the resistance area of possible downward correction for this pair is strong enough. As can be seen, the price started its decline from the FE 138.2% level, which means that the required conditions were met. This example confirms that FE 138.2% performs well even when it is not a key level for the specific currency pair.

6.1.5. FE 150%

FE 150% properties are similar to those of FE 138.2% and both refer to strong support/resistance levels. Another similarity with 150% FE is observed: FE 138.2% is a key level for the specific group of currency pairs. In these pairs, EUR stands as a first member, i.e., EUR/USD, EUR/JPY, EUR/CHF, EUR/GBP, etc. Here the FE 150% level does not require confirmation to decide on entering the market, since in most cases it acts as key support or resistance.

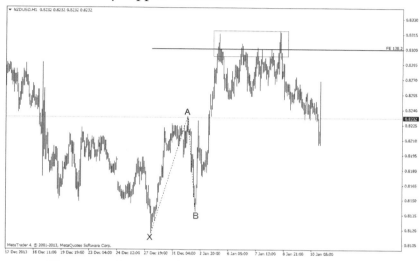

Figure 135. Projection level FE 150 %, EUR/USD, Weekly

Figure 136. Projection level FE 150 %, EUR/JPY, H1

In Figure 135, the projection is built on the first wave of long-term uptrend for the EUR/USD pair, Weekly timeframe. During formation of the upward trend, a key resistance level of 150% FE was reached. As can be seen from the chart, the price did not exceed this level, but instead formed an extremum, reversed, and formed subsequently a new downward trend.

A similar example is demonstrated in Figure 136. During formation of the short-term downward trend, the EUR/JPY pair reached a key resistance level of 150% FE on Fibonacci projection. After that, a sharp reversal in price and the subsequent uprise was observed. The FE 150% property, as a key level for EUR/JPY pair, was important to this process.

Another example of the projection is demonstrated below. Here, the FE 150% acted as support, but failed to reverse the price properly. Projection is built on the USD/JPY pair and FE 150% does not act as key support for this pair.

Figure 137. Projection level FE 150 %, USD/JPY, H4

6.1.6 FE 161.8% and FE 200%

The final levels of Fibonacci projection – FE 161.8% and FE 200% - are the most important to analysis and trading and they are widely used in composite clusters. These refer to the strongest support/resistance levels in Fibonacci projection, regardless of the type of financial asset. Under the Comprehensive Fibonacci analysis, these levels are given top priority, since they form the most significant price reversals, independent of the time scale considered (H1 to Monthly timeframes).

Figure 138. Projection levels FE 161.8% and FE 200%, USD/CHF, H4

Figure 139. Projection levels FE 161.8% and FE 200%, EUR/USD, H1

Examples of interactions between key projection levels and the price are demonstrated in figures above.

In Figure 138, the projection is built on an upward trend of the USD/CHF currency pair. After a steady rise, the price reached FE 161.8%. Here the price stayed for a while and formed a local extremum at this level. Then the upward movement continued and the final level of FE 200% was reached. Finally, the price reversed and started downward immediately after reaching key resistance.

In Figure 139, projection is built on a short-term downward trend for EUR/USD and you can see that here the FE 161.8% level performed stronger than 200% FE. Price reversal from FE 161.8% was significant, whereas reversal from the FE 200% level was stopped by the same FE 161.8% level, which acted as resistance in this case (prior to that it acted as support).

A final example of the price behavior at key levels is demonstrated in Figure 140.

Figure 140. Projection levels FE 161.8% and FE 200%, AUD/USD, Daily

The figure above shows the projection built on the first and second uptrend waves for AUD/USD. In this case, successive hitting of resistance key levels led to the price reversal, from each level – i.e., twice. Reversal at FE 161.8% was less strong while at FE 200% the price reversed significantly and changed into the downward trend afterwards.

The properties of Fibonacci projection levels refer to important features of this tool and should be considered in trading. The known properties allow us to predict accurately whether and how a certain level will act.

Fibonacci projection levels provide no clues about the strength of price reversal. With view of trading, they are uninformative on the purpose of a transaction when attempting to catch a bounce from the level. Under the Comprehensive Fibonacci analysis, a projection is applied in combination with auxiliary tools, to provide the basis for transactions. The main objective of Fibonacci projection is to determine the level or the area of price reversal. A transaction to buy or sell is opened with use of the CFA tools and in the area defined by the projection.

Our intention to start with the review of properties of the projection levels, instead of methods of constructing the tool, is not accidental. The principles of constructing projection are not too complicated. At the same time, certain features should be considered when building Fibonacci projection. These features aim ultimately at maximizing the projection efficiency as a trading tool.

6.2. Breakout at 200% FE

According to the list of projection levels presented in the previous chapter, the final key is 200% FE. Surely, extra levels could be added afterwards by using Fibonacci ratios, but these are unnecessary. The matter is that properties of all levels, up to FE 200%, are already described and tested in trading practice.

The price often goes beyond the FE 200% level. Despite its strength as support or resistance, this level can be broken and in such cases, price movements cannot be analyzed with projection levels, though this analysis is needed in most situations.

When FE 200% is broken by the price, projection should be rebuilt on the next wave of the trend or correction. This is not too complicated and the principles of rebuilding at FE 200% breakdown are exemplified below.

Figure 141. Fibonacci projection, USD/JPY, Daily

In Figure 141, Fibonacci projection is built on the USD/JPY downtrend. Note the accurate performance of levels during the downtrend: FE 100 %, FE 138.2% (a key for this currency pair), FE 161.8%, and FE 200%. Finally, the USD/JPY pair broke the FE 200% level and in this situation the projection should be reconstructed. The principle for rebuilding projection is demonstrated in Figure 142.

Figure 142. Rebuilding projection from AB onto A'B' wave, USD/JPY, Daily

When rebuilding any projection, the point X (the starting point of price movement) remains in place, whereas points A and B move to the next wave of price movement. Figure 142 shows that projection was shifted downward onto the next rising wave, as compared with the initial construction of the tool on points AB; the point X remained in the same place. Thus, the rebuilt projection is based on points X, A', and B', instead of points X, A, and B used previously.

This principle allows for shifting the rebuilt Fibo levels farther in the direction of price movement. After the breakdown of FE 200%, projection levels appeared in new areas (unobserved earlier). Figure 145 shows that after rebuilding the price reached the key support level, FE 161.8%. Figure 143 shows development of this situation, as follows.

After reaching FE 161.8% from the rebuilt projection, an extremum was formed. Then followed the price reversal, from downward to upward movement, and later the price could rise significantly. If the projection rebuilding was not performed, we were unable to specify locations of support/resistance levels. This example clearly shows the need of projection rebuilding after the FE 200% breakdown.

Figure 143. Price reversal at FE 161.8%, the rebuilt projection, USD/JPY, Daily

The next example demonstrates the projection rebuilding, Figs. 144-146.

Figure 144. Fibonacci projection, EUR/USD, H4

Fibonacci projection is built on the EUR/USD uptrend (Figure 144 over the points X, A, and B. This construction method is ideal for tracing the price movements: projection levels performed well in the upward process. Note also the price reversals from the marked levels. We can notice that the price moves in accordance with all properties of Fibo levels: in some cases the level acts as a key support/resistance, in the others – it is triggered only by a breakdown and the price reversal. Figure 145 demonstrates the already broken FE 200% and, therefore, the projection needs to be rebuilt.

Figure 145. Rebuilding projection from AB onto A'B' wave, EUR/USD, H4

The process of projection rebuilding is demonstrated in Figure 145. Point X always stays in place and points A and B are moved/shifted. They are rebuilt onto the next downward wave in the trend and a new projection is built over the correct points X, A', and B'.

A number of small waves were observed between price segments A:B and A':B', but we should select only the evident price movements for rebuilding the projection and disregard minor upward or downward price waves.

Figure 146. Price reversal at FE 161.8%, the rebuilt projection, EUR/USD, H4

After rebuilding Fibonacci projection, the price started its move, according to the updated support/resistance levels. Figure 146 demonstrates a good performance of resistance levels, FE 138.2% (a strong but not key level for the EUR/USD) and FE 161.8%. A remarkable fact is that, despite the spike was formed at FE 161.8%, the reversal occurred directly at FE 150%. Following the strong rise, the price formed an extremum at FE 161.8% and closing prices remained at FE 150% - the key level for EUR/USD.

The final example for rebuilding projection is demonstrated below.

Figure 147. Fibonacci projection, EUR/GBP, H1

Figure 147 demonstrates building a projection on the EUR/GBP hourly chart. Projection levels performed well and even at the time of publication of strong fundamental data, FE 61.8% held the price, in line with its properties. At the moment, the FE 200% level is already broken and the projection needs to be rebuilt.

Figure 148. Rebuilding projection from AB to onto A'B' wave, EUR/GBP, H1

Rebuilding projection, according to the standard schematic plan, is demonstrated in Figure 148. Points A and B are shifted onto the next downtrend wave and the projection is based upon points X, A', and B'. In the future, the price will respond to levels of the rebuilt projection, as is shown in Figure 149.

Figure 149. Price reversal at FE 150% and FE 61.8%, EUR/GBP, H1

The figure above shows that levels of the rebuilt projection performed well. The EUR/GBP pair hit the FE 150% projection level (key for this currency pair) and reversed. Later, the upward price move led this pair to the FE 61.8% level, where it acted, quite predictably, as resistance. The price made a pronounced reversal at this level and proceeded further in a downtrend.

Rebuilding projection after the FE 200% breakdown helps to estimate future price changes. This Fibonacci tool should be moved after each breakdown of the final level. When rebuilding, the point X always remains in place, whereas points A and B are moved onto the next wave of price movement.

6.3. Relationship with the retracement construction

When a trader takes the first steps in this method of construction and application of the projection, he asks, if there exists a construction pattern for Fibonacci retracement, consisting of five tools of different time scale, and whether such pattern is available for the projection? Should we build the projection in a similar way, for five different timeframes, from Monthly to H1?

Before we answer this question, the following notion should be clarified. Projection, as a tool for indicating support or resistance levels, is built on the price movement, which should be evaluated.

Here's what it means: the vast majority of trading situations in the currency market is described by Fibonacci retracement in detail. It allows us to determine support/resistance levels and internal correction patterns – these two factors are quite sufficient for successful trading. In this respect, Fibonacci projection can be called an auxiliary tool, needed exclusively for identifying composite clusters (unlike retracement, we do not trade upon the Fibonacci projection alone).

Therefore, projection is constructed whenever needed. There is no need in building five Fibonacci projections on different timeframes. But when we need to define a support/resistance cluster in a specific price movement, projection could and should be built.

Moreover, Fibonacci retracement is constructed on the already formed price movement (in other words – upon the price history), in order to work with the correction. Projection is extended both on the correction and on the developing trend, where retracement cannot be built so far.

Let's take a look at the example below.

Figure 150. Upward 4-H trend, EUR/USD, Daily

Figure 150 demonstrates the recent price situation for the EUR/USD currency pair. Fibonacci retracement for evaluating downward correction is plotted on the chart, according to the pattern and building algorithm.

In this situation, there are two possibilities to construct a projection – on an upward trend, over the points X1, A1, and B1, and on the correction, over the points X2, A2, and B2. If we use the first option, it will result in a projection that evaluates this trend. Despite the fact that it performed well and the price reversal at the maximum (point X2) occurred precisely at FE 200% of this projection, this construction is outdated and hence, useless. At the moment, a downward correction is formed and we need a projection within this movement. Accordingly, this projection (Figure 150) should be constructed over the points X2, A2, and B2. The levels of this projection, in combination with the retracement levels, will indicate the support areas. If the EUR/USD takes further drop, these correction areas will be helpful for opening transactions.

This factor must be considered when deciding where to build the projection. For the best trading opportunities, you need to understand what price movement is to be estimated by the projection and select carefully the trend or correction to be projected.

6.4. Unsuitable points for building projection

In certain market situations, building projection is impossible. Generally, this happens when projected price movements are either too small or too long, so projecting becomes meaningless.

Let's take a look at the figure below.

Figure 151. Unsuitable point for building projection, EUR/USD, H1

Figure 151 raises questions, others than those respective to the X point. The starting point of price movement is clearly visible, but then everything gets confusing. If we build a projection over points X, A1, and B1, the levels would be located too close to each other and therefore, useless. So, such construction is unsuitable in this situation.

If we build a projection over points X, A2, and B2, the levels of projection will be far below the current price changes and such projection is unable to evaluate the downward price movement. Therefore, this building method is not suitable, too.

What shall we do? The answer is simple: nothing. If the price-derived movements are unsuitable for constructing projection, it should not be built at all. This is an auxiliary tool and, if impossible to be built under certain market conditions – just skip it. When there are no apparent first and second projection waves – there is no projection.

Figure 152. Projection built on the upward trend, USD/CHF, H4

Figure 152 demonstrates an example of constructing projection. The need of rebuilding is clearly visible on the chart. Projection worked perfectly during the upward process but needs rebuilding if FE 200% is broken. Projection rebuilding is shown in Figure 152.

Figure 153. Projection rebuilding on USD/CHF, H4

The USD/CHF has only one option to rebuild the projection, which is to move it from points A and B to points A' and B' (Figure 153). However, under such rebuilding the X:A wave is very long and all projection levels are located far above the current price. This could possibly be good for the future situation, if the price gets much higher, but at the moment, such construction is useless and therefore, unneeded.

6.5. Preferred building option

The examples above indicate clearly that projection is always constructed from the developed extremum point, after the price reversal. Construction is always started either from the point of starting the trend, or from the point of starting the correction (X). This point is retained when rebuilding the projection, while points A and B are moved.

The common method of constructing projection adopted, for example, in the EWA, is construction on multiple waves, with view of defining the level of tentative end of the next wave. Under this approach, projection is built as follows:

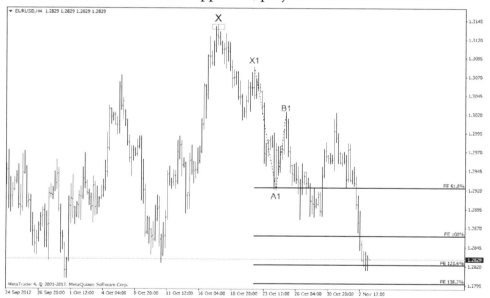

Figure 154. Constructing projections on internal downtrend waves, EUR/USD, H4

Figure 154 demonstrates an example of constructing projections used as references in CFA books. For instance, in Elliott Wave Analysis these constructions allow traders to determine approximate levels where the wave (pulse or correction) end is expected. In this method, the starting point X is ignored and projection is built over points X1, A1, and B1.

Such construction method is appropriate when the end of a specific wave is predicted, but under Comprehensive Fibonacci analysis, projection is applied to reveal support and resistance levels of the possible price reversal. In this case, we need to know where the price reversal is expected and where to enter the market profitably.

Therefore, in accordance with the CFA rules of constructing projection, the tool (Figure 154) should be built from the point X, instead of X1. In this case, projection will evaluate the entire price movement rather than any particular wave. Here, the trader can determine the most important trading extremes for gaining greater profit.

I do not recommend building projection "inward" of the price movement, because in this case, the analysis is based on a single detail instead of the whole situation. As a result, the integral picture of price changes is overlooked and the trader focuses on a separate price segment, which may affect adversely his decision to enter the market.

6.6. Clustered projection building

In conclusion, we need to mention an exception to the rules discussed earlier. Let us turn to Figure 155.

Figure 155. Two projections built on the GBP/USD uptrend, Daily

Figure 155 demonstrates construction of two Fibonacci projections. You may notice that the second projection built over points X2, A2, B2, contradicts with my earlier statement – since it is built "inward" of the price movement. This and similar situations represent an important exception.

The fact is that these two projections refer to different time intervals. In other words, projection X1:A1:B1 evaluates the entire GBP/USD uptrend in this chart, whereas projection X2:A2:B2 was built after a deep internal correction of the trend and evaluates a shorter-term rise, i.e., an internal short-term trend. Thus, we have two upward movements: the long- and short-term, and in this situation we can build projection on both segments of the entire trend. Figure 156 demonstrates results of such clustered building:

Figure 156. Resistance clusters in clustered projection building, GBP/USD, Daily

The figure above shows that the levels of two projections form simple clusters of resistance (marked on the chart). Note that in each cluster testing the price moved to the correction. These movements can be used in forming short-term sales of GBP/USD and thus, diversify the GBP/USD purchases within the uptrend.

This represents the only situation when projection should be built within the price movement. Such situations are not uncommon in the foreign exchange market. In cases when different segments of the trend belong to different time intervals, we can build several projections to define simple support/resistance clusters (in the same way as for clustered construction of retracement).

Chapter 7
Fibonacci extension: two types of tools

The final tool used in Comprehensive Fibonacci analysis is extension. Depending on the method of construction, two types are distinguished: extension of type I and extension of type II.

This Fibonacci tool is applied to define additional support/resistance levels and it can be built in situations where the pattern of price movements is not fully clear. It is particularly convenient in situations when constructing Fibonacci retracement or projection is not feasible.

This tool can be referred to as an auxiliary but it is needed in great variety of situations and therefore Fibonacci Extensions of type I and II are applied equally with other tools of Comprehensive Fibonacci analysis.

7.1. Extension of type I

The figure below demonstrates schematic plan of constructing Fibonacci Extension of type I. This method makes possible finding additional support/resistance levels, which are not considered as key levels, but represent a good barrier for the price. These levels play a major role in composite clusters.

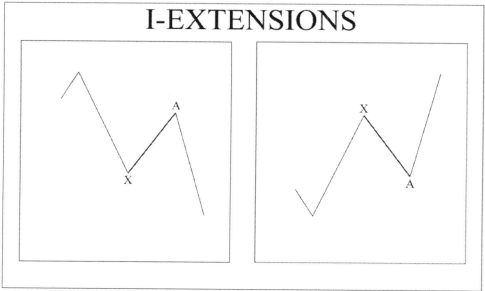

Figure 157. Construction of Fibonacci Extension-I

Fibonacci Extension represents two additional retracement levels – 127.2% and 161.8%. Up to this moment, we discussed internal retracement levels only, from 0%

to 100%. Two external levels will be important for this extension.

This type of extension is based on internal trend waves and if a trader is skilled in constructing Fibonacci projection, no difficulties will arise with constructing Fibonacci Extension-I.

Let's take a look at Figure 158, which exemplifies construction of Extension- I.

Figure 158. Fibonacci Extension-1, EUR/USD, H4

The chart demonstrates a downward trend for the EUR/USD pair, where Extension-I is built, in line with the rules, on the internal wave, the interval X:A; the 127.2% and 161.8% levels are located below the price. In this case, Extension-I acts as support and Figure 158 shows that as soon as the price hit the 127.2% level, the downward movement reversed immediately to an upward vector.

Figure 159 demonstrates the principle of building extension on the internal correction wave. The downward correction movement on the USD/JPY currency pair formed an internal upward wave X:A and after its completion Extension-I could be built. Following a strong decline, correction price reached 161.8% level and then reversed immediately and raced up. This movement could be leveraged by buying USD/JPY from the161.8% level. The price immediately broke the 127.2% level, which acted as resistance, so entering into a transaction at this level would have been risky.

Figure 159. Fibonacci Extension-I, USD/JPY, H4

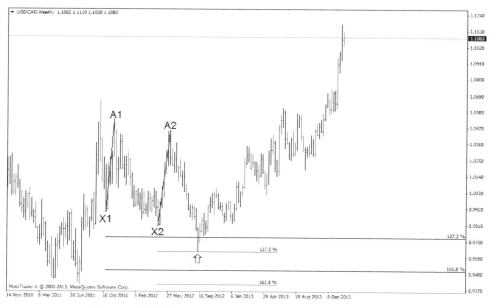

Figure 160. Fibonacci Extension-I, USD/CAD, Weekly

Figure 160 demonstrates construction of two long-term Fibonacci projections on the weekly chart, USD/CAD. This example shows that in certain situations two extensions can be built instead of one. To do this, we need to have two internal waves in a trend or in correction. Such situation is demonstrated for the USD/CAD pair.

As is seen in the figure, the price reached the 127.2% level from two Fibonacci Extensions, and it is from this area that the upward price movement started and finally turned into a new long-term trend for the USD/CAD.

If only one extension tool is available, we cannot predict where the reversal will occur – at 127.2% or 161.8% level. It should be noted that under Comprehensive Fibonacci analysis, extension is not applied as a standalone tool, but only in combination with retracement or extension. At this step, it is important to specify the method of constructing extension and then we will discuss composite clusters.

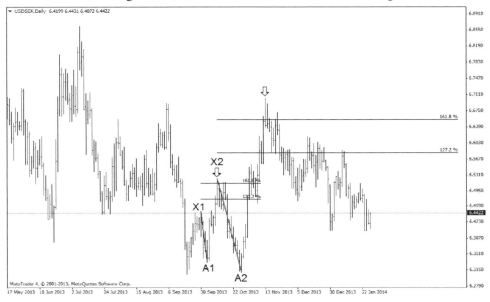

Figure 161. Fibonacci Extension-I, USD/SEK, Daily

Figure 161 demonstrates an example of constructing two Fibonacci projections on different internal waves. The price constructed upon X1:A1 projection reached the 161.8% level and then decreased, thereby forming the second wave X2:A2. After constructing the second extension on X2:A2 wave, the price reached the 161.8% level and started in decline, which has developed subsequently into a new downward trend.

A final example of constructing Extension-I is shown in Figure 162.

Figure 162. Comparison between Fibonacci projection and Extension-I, GBP/USD, H1

In the above GBP/USD chart, in addition to Extension-I, Fibonacci projection is plotted by points HH:X:A. Extension is built on the internal wave X:A. Note that the resultant projection is "deep" and the price has not reached the 100% FE level. This is explained by the fact that points used for plotting projection were not too good, but here we have no other options to build a tool. As compared with the projection, Extension-I performed in this situation more precisely, the price reached the 127.2% level, reversed and the GBP/USD pair soon started upward.

7.2. Fibonacci Extension-II

Fibonacci Extensions of type I and type II differ between themselves by methods of construction the tool upon the price chart, as well as the analysis of price changes using extensions. Extension-I helps in defining additional support/resistance levels and two auxiliary Fibonacci levels, 127.2% and 161.8% are used for this purpose. Extension-II is used to define the price area, where the price can stop and reverse. Thus, the price area between the 127.2% and 161.8% levels is more significant to Extension-II, rather than levels as such. They can act as support or resistance, but a buffer zone between them is more important for this Fibonacci tool.

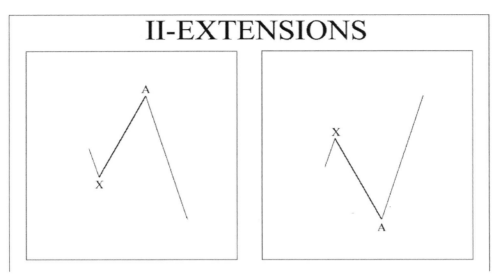

Figure 163. Construction of Fibonacci Extension-II

Figure 163 demonstrates schematic plan for constructing the tool. This type is built on the last wave that is formed prior to price reversal, instead of the internal trend wave, or correction. After the wave is formed, the highest high or lowest low should be formed on the asset, depending on the direction of motion, and the market would reverse. Once this has happened, Extension-II is built on the final rise/ fall wave, from min to max.

Figure 164 demonstrates an example of building Extension-II on the EUR/USD chart.

Figure 164. Extension-II, EUR/USD, H4

Pay attention to the construction of Extension-II on the EUR/USD pair. After a prolonged upward trend, the price formed the highest high in point A, and then went down for some time. The last upward price segment (X:A) was selected for constructing the extension and the area between the 127.2% and 161.8% levels acted as buffer for the price. The EUR/USD pair entered the buffer zone briefly, but soon "broke surface". From the standpoint of support/resistance, the price in this area is subjected to great pressure and that is why the price "floats away" from this area.

Figure 165. Extension-II, USD/CAD, Daily

In Figure 165, Fibonacci Extension-II is built on the last X:A segment of downward trend for the USD/CAD. Upward correction reached the area between the 127.2% and 161.8% levels and after that started downward, failing to go beyond the resistance buffer defined by extension.

At times, price movements in the market prevent unambiguous selection of the point to build Extension-II. Typically, in such situations there is no straightforward maximum or minimum to build a tool. If the last segment of the trend is unclear for a certain financial asset, the tool is better left alone, and the trader should address another, clearer situation. The shift of the questioned buffer zone can be caused by controversy of construction point and further compromise results of the analysis. Therefore, the same as with other tools in Comprehensive Fibonacci analysis, if you cannot build the actual Extension-II – just skip it.

An example of this situation is shown in Figure 166.

Figure 166. Fibonacci Extension-II, NZD/USD

In this example we can see that the last segment of the uptrend for NZD/USD pair was very strong, with no apparent internal downward corrections. If Extension-II is constructed as shown in the figure (through points X and A), extension levels would be placed very low and therefore, have little relevance to the current price movement on the NZD/USD pair. At the current price level projection is useless, but if NZD/USD would later reach the buffer zone on this extension, it would act as support. Let us look at the figure below.

Figure 167. Reaching the extension buffer zone, NZD/USD, H4

Figure 167 demonstrates the current price changes for the NZD/USD pair. The price reached the area of Extension-II and reversed; its direction changed from downward to upward.

When preparing this section, I discovered a trading situation for the AUD/USD pair, when the price reached the resistance buffer zone on H1 timeframe upon Extension-II (Figure 168).

In this situation, we observed a general downward trend and upward correction, which could end just in the buffer zone of Extension- II, so it was decided to open a transaction to sell AUD/USD. Since the direct entry from the resistance zone failed and the profit/loss ratio in this transaction was not up to par (55 points potential losses against 70 points potential gains), the transaction was opened at minimal volume of 1 lot. Stop-loss order was set just above the 161.8% level, upon the expectation that the price would remain within the resistance buffer zone and take-profit order was set at 14.6% from 1-H trend retracement (Figure 169).

Figure 168. AUD/USD sale from resistance zone of Extension-II, H1

Figure 169. Total sale for AUD/USD, H1

This transaction was not perfect, because it missed an opportunity to sell the pair from the resistance zone, by 30 points higher. However, the transaction ended successfully: immediately after the entry into the market, AUD/USD started downward trend and take-profit order was reached in 14 hours. Profit on the transaction, net of fees, made 956 dollars[21].

A careful reader may notice that in Figure 169, AUD/USD formed a bullish IP2 pattern upon Fibonacci retracement, after declining from the 38.2% to 14.6% level. This fact had no relation to projection, but it was decided to use this pattern for trading. We will discuss it in more details in Chapter 11.

A final example of building Fibonacci Extension-II is demonstrated in Figure 170.

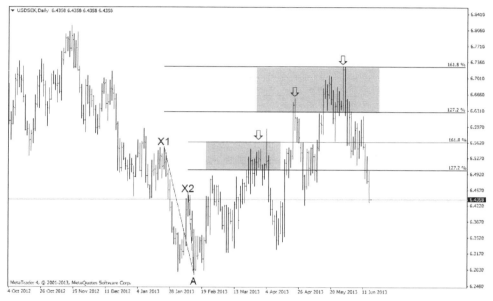

Figure 170. Two Fibonacci Extensions-II, USD/SEK, Daily

The figure above demonstrates simultaneous construction of two Fibonacci Extensions of the second type. Segment X2:A refers to a short-term 4-H trend, therefore, extension constructed on this segment pointed to a short-term resistance buffer zone that performed flawlessly. Extension constructed on X1:A segment refers to a longer-term daily trend and, accordingly, the price reversal from the buffer zone between Fibonacci levels will be more significant and lasting. In such situations, two tools can be built d simultaneously and the most important thing here is to remember, what timeframe is linked to this or that tool and thus avoid confusion.

When getting familiarized with the property of Extension-II, the reader may ask: how to use this property in trading? The mere fact that the price can reverse from the area between levels is important but even so, the entry point should be defined more precisely. Let's do it next.

---

21. Cost per pip – 15 USD.

SECTION II.
Comprehensive Fibonacci analysis

Chapter 8
*Composite support/resistance clusters
as the basis for trading with CFA*

Joint application of Fibonacci retracement, extension, and projection allows the trader to determine price levels, where the price reversal can take place. However, we do not need all CFA tools to be applied to every market situation. More often, they are applied pairwise, e.g., retracement + projection, retracement + extension, or extension + projection. Despite the fact that these tools have similar properties, the methods for their construction are quite different. In situations when building retracement is not possible, the trader can apply extension and projection. And when the market projection could not be constructed, the key areas of support/resistance are estimated with combination of retracement and extension.

A search for composite clusters, i.e., clusters consisting of different CFA tool levels, is intended for one purpose only – to find the price level, which triggers its reversal.

Such key cluster can be defined upon the level properties of the tools. As we already know, in the CFA tools some levels are stronger, some are weaker, and some refer to the key levels (the strongest levels of support/resistance). With due regard to these properties, as well as relying on correct construction of Fibonacci tools, the trader can determine the point of entry into the market and the direction of price movement after reaching the composite cluster.

First, let's get familiarized with three search options for composite clusters.

8.1. Retracement + projection

The first method for defining a composite cluster is the most common. To determine the composite cluster, we use Fibonacci retracement and projection. Combined properties of both tools provide an integral picture of price movements.

Let's take a look at Figure 171.

Figure 171. Composite support cluster, EUR/ USD, H4

In Figure 1, the support cluster was defined by constructing Fibonacci retracement and projection. We can notice that throughout the correction process, from 0% to 50% level, the price did not form IP. To determine, whether a cluster existed at this level, the projection was plotted via the points A: B: C. A strong support level, FE 138.2% was found around the 50% level. Thus, we discovered a composite cluster 50% + FE 138.2%, after hitting it, the price immediately went upward (Figure 172).

Figure 172. Upturn in the price from the composite support cluster, EUR/ USD, H4

How to transact in this situation? After entering into purchase from the support cluster, a stop-loss order could be placed under the FE 161.8% level, and a take-profit order – at the 23.6% level. Thus, placing the take-profit order would encourage formation of IP3 pattern. Since no price IPs were observed before it, formation of IP3 pattern was highly probable.

The figure below demonstrates another example of defining a composite cluster.

Figure 173. Composite resistance cluster, AUD/ USD, H4

Figure 173 shows that after building retracement (X: A) and projection (A: B: C), three clusters of resistance were defined: a weak FE 100% + 38.2% cluster and two key clusters, FE 123.6% + 50% and FE 161.8% + 61.8%. The second key cluster resistance is more important, as is consists of two key levels. Such clusters often act as the price "magnet". However, IPs were not formed during correction, so we could not yet assume reaching the 61.8% level and the available level-based cluster (because 50% is a key resistance). To start with, the price went down after hitting the composite cluster FE 123.6% + 50%, which justified entering into a transaction to sell (Figure 174). The sales target was 23.6%, where the price formed IP3.

Figure 174. Downturn in the price from the cluster and IP3 formation, AUD/USD, H4

In addition to the FE 123.6% + 50% cluster, one more key composite cluster was observed at 61.8% retracement. Therefore, IP3 pattern could be used for entering a purchase transaction. In this case, 61.8% + FE 161.8% cluster made the target level and the stop-loss order was placed at the 0% level, according to the pattern rules. In the future, the price increased and the final key cluster was reached (Figure 175).

Figure 175. Reaching the key resistance cluster, AUD/USD, H4

A final example of finding the cluster with retracement and projection is demonstrated in Figures 176-179.

Figure 176. Composite clusters of support, USD/ CAD, H4

Figure 176 shows that by constructing projection and retracement, we got 2 support clusters: FE 100% + 38.2% and the key cluster FE 61.8 + 61.8%. The first cluster is strong, but buying assets from it would be risky, because the price has a more important target – the key composite cluster at the 61.8% level. In this situation, the best strategy is to wait and watch the price behavior.

Figure 177. Resistance clusters + IP1, USD/CAD, H4

Figure 177 shows that in the uptrend from the support cluster, the price reached 9% level and, thus, IP1 appeared on USD/CAD. Two clusters are seen in the area of 9% level: FE 123.6% + 14.6% (a weak cluster) and FE 138.2% + 9% (a key cluster). So, in addition to IP1, the resistance cluster was discovered at Level 2, which would prevent further upward movement. This makes an excellent opportunity to enter a transaction to sell. Here, placing stop-loss and take-profit orders is made according to IP1 rules. The target level for IP1 is 50%, but the price could reach the key support cluster FE 61.8% + 61.8% after the breakout of the 50 % level.

Development of this situation is demonstrated in Figure 178.

Figure 178. Reaching the price target level of 50% and the key cluster, USD/CAD, H4

As can be seen from this chart, a strong drop off the 38.2% allowed the price to penetrate the 50% level and immediately reach the support cluster. In this situation, we can observe good results from combining Fibonacci retracement and projection.

8.2. Retracement + extension-I

The next option of finding clusters by retracement and extension-I can be used in situations when Fibonacci projection is inapplicable for some reason. Despite the fact that extension-I contains only 2 Fibonacci levels, they are quite sufficient for finding key support/resistance clusters provided that retracement is already built on the chart.

Figure 179 shows an example of joint construction of retracement and extension-I.

Figure 179. Composite support cluster, EUR/USD, H1

In Figure 179, the composite cluster was identified using retracement and Fibo-nacci extension-I. Two support clusters are visible in the chart (50% + 127.2% and 61.8% + 161.8%). Given the fact that IPs are absent throughout the correction (the price did not reach 14.6%, so there is no IP2), the key 50% + 127.2% cluster can act as the support, so that EUR/USD hits this level, reverses, and goes up to at least 23.6%. The stop-loss order in this case should be placed under the lower support cluster. Development of this situation is shown in Figure 180.

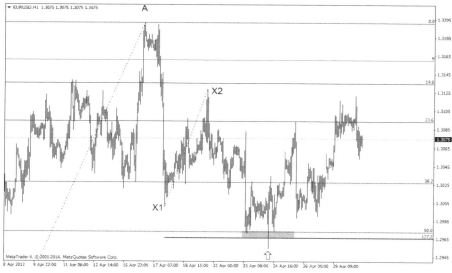

Figure 180. Upturn in the price after reaching the support cluster, EUR/USD, H1

Let us analyze the following example of combined application of retracement and extension-I.

Figure 181. Composite clusters of support, GBP/JPY, H1

Figure 181 demonstrates two clusters of support, which were found by constructing retracement and extension-I. We also see here IP1 pattern (23.6% - 9%), which targets the 50% level. If we missed entering into a transaction at 9%, to take advantage of IP1, we could buy GBP/JPY from the composite cluster 50% + 127.2%. In this situation, stop-loss is placed under the lower cluster 61.8% + 161.8. If the price rises up to 14.6%, we will get IP2 pattern targeted at the lower cluster (Figure 182).

Figure 182. IP2 pattern, GBP/JPY, H1

Figure 182 demonstrates that after the upturn from the first composite cluster, IP2 pattern was formed. This makes a good opportunity to sell GBP/JPY with a target at the 61.8% level. By this moment, buying from the 50% + 127.2% cluster must be closed.

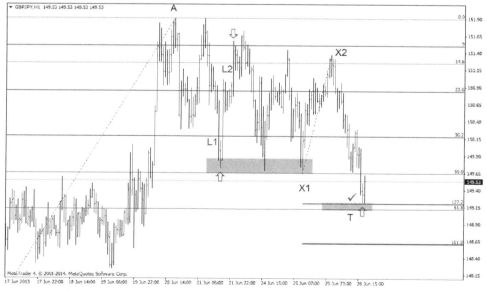

Figure 183. The price reaches the 61.8% + 127.2% composite cluster

Figure 183 shows that the cluster at 50% prevented the price downtrend for a long time and IP3 pattern was formed during correction, with the same target level of 61.8%. Finally, the price reached this level, or rather reached the cluster detected by constructing extension-I on the price-nearest correction segment X1:X2. The fact that the price did not touch the 61.8% level does not mean that the retracement target was missed. Reaching 61.8% was prevented by 127.2% level, and therefore, we can conclude that correction was completed.

And this is not the whole story. Since a set of patterns was formed within correction process and the price reached the target support cluster, correction may be considered complete. Therefore, we can open a transaction to buy the GBP/JPY pair from the cluster 61.8% + 127.2%. The target of this transaction is to get the price to increase over the 0% level (with expectation of the continued upward trend). Figure 184 shows development of this situation.

Figure 184. Upturn in the price after reaching the target support cluster, GBP/JPY, H1

As can be seen from the figure above, the GBP/JPY pair started upward immediately after reaching the last composite support cluster and gained 270 points in 4 days.

Thus, by applying the CFA tools, upon understanding the price behavior in correction and proper construction and application of Fibonacci tools, an ordinary price correction on the GBP/JPY currency pair turned into a great profit: in 7 trading days, the profit from all possible operations amounted to almost 950 points!

The final example of combined application of retracement and extension of the first type is shown in Figures 185-187.

Figure 185. Composite clusters of resistance, AUD/USD, H1

Figure 186. Downturn in the price from the resistance cluster, AUD/USD, H1

In Figure 185, retracement and extension-I were built on the AUD/USD currency pair. Here we can see two clusters of resistance and the presence of IP2 pattern in correction. This is a familiar situation and it means that the price can form an extremum on the 50% + 127.2% cluster, but finally the price will reach the target 61.8% level, which is included in the 61.8% + 161.8% cluster.

Figure 186 shows the price downtrend from the 50% + 127.2% cluster. This is a good reason to sell an asset with the target of 50% and a stop-loss order beyond the upper cluster. Upon reaching the 23.6% level, transactions to sell should be closed against opening transactions to buy, with a target at the 61.8% + 161.8% cluster (IP3 appeared).

Figure 187. Reaching the target composite cluster, AUD/USD, H1

Eventually, the price reached the composite cluster 61.8% + 161.8% (Figure 187). It dropped slightly after entry into the AUD/USD purchase, but still did not reach the stop-loss level, as placed by IP3 rules.

Relying on our knowledge about internal retracement patterns, this situation could be limited to a transaction at IP2 and 61.8% target. Then another purchase could be opened upon IP3. Using Fibonacci extension-I, another transaction could be opened within this correction: to sell AUD/USD from the 50% level, because the key composite resistance cluster was located at this level.

Thus, integrated application of the tools and comprehensive assessment of the price correction provides for much more trading situations and that is why composite clusters are so important in trading.

8.3. Projection + Extension-I

The above examples show application of the CFA tools to the FOREX and are related to correction.

In case of joint application of projection and extension-I, we can find composite clusters within the developing trend. Let's take a look at Figure 188.

Figure 188. Composite support cluster, GBP/USD, H1

In the figure above, the support cluster FE 138.2% + 127.2% is identified by point wise projection X: A: B, and extension-I (X1: A1). Both these levels are strong levels of support; therefore, we can expect the upturn in the price after reaching this composite cluster.

Figure 189. Price reversal after reaching the resistance cluster, GBP/USD, H1

Figure 189 shows that the GBP/USD pair started upward immediately after reaching the composite support cluster. The feasible upturn from the cluster should be used in trading by opening a transaction to buy GBP/USD pair from a combination of levels FE 138.2% + 127.2%.

Figure 190. Composite support cluster, USD/JPY

Figure 190 presents a similar example of a composite support cluster. Two support clusters on USD/JPY were identified with projection and extension-I. Figure 190 shows that the price has first reached FE 161.8% + 127.2%. Since it is the key cluster, we could enter the market to buy. Development of this situation is shown in Figure 191.

Figure 191. Reaching both composite clusters, USD/JPY, H4

Following a minor uptrend from the FE 161.8% + 127.2% cluster, a downtrend resumed, and the price eventually reached the final composite support cluster, FE 200% + 161.8% (Figure 191). Immediately after that the USD/JPY pair went upward and increased by more than 200 points in the end.

The first support cluster was less strong than the second; however, entering into a transaction to buy from the first cluster and the standard placement of stop-loss order after the second cluster resulted in stop-loss failure. Further rise made purchases of USD/JPY profitable.

The final example of combined application of projection and extension-I is shown in Figures 192 and 193.

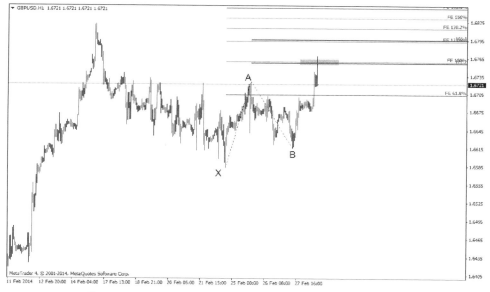

Figure 192. Composite resistance cluster, GBP/USD, H1

Figure 193. Downturn in the price from the resistance cluster, GBP/USD, H1

Figures 192 and 193 illustrate building projections by points X: A: B and extension-I by points A:B. Composite clusters obtained from both tools indicated the areas of resistance appropriate for entering a transaction to sell. Upon reaching the first cluster, FE 100% + 127.2%, the price attempted to break it but failed; further the GBP/USD pair dropped by 100 points.

8.4. Selection of priority cluster

Previously we discussed all CFA tools but did not mention the extension of second type, as part of clusters. However, this tool is very important when dealing with several clusters of support/resistance.

In the examples presented previously in this chapter we have often seen one, sometimes two or three clusters. In such situations, the choice of priority cluster to enter into a transaction is made upon indirect indicators (e.g., the presence of IP in correction).

Application of extension-I can simplify selection of priority cluster, makes it more systemic and excludes the need to explore correction.

Let's take a look at the first example, Figures 194-196.

Figure 194. Two clusters of support, EUR/USD, H4

Figure 194 shows two composite support clusters found with use of projection and extension-I. In this situation, the trader faces the task of selecting priority cluster, i.e., the one to enter into a transaction to buy EUR/USD.

When selection is made between several clusters, we need to construct Extension of the second type. The cluster, which falls into the buffer zone between the levels 127.2% and 161.8%, will be a priority. A decision to open a transaction to buy or sell is made upon this cluster defined by extension-II.

Let's take a look at Figures 195 and 196.

Figure 195. Construction of extension-II and selection of priority cluster, EUR/USD, H4

Figure 196. Upturn in the price from the selected support cluster, EUR/USD, H4

In Figure 195, we can see a buffer zone between the levels 127.2% and 161.8%. The upper resistance cluster fell into this buffer zone. This means that this cluster is a priority for trading and the market should be entered from this area of support. The lower cluster is located outside the buffer zone and, therefore, is less important. After hitting the priority cluster, EUR/USD displayed a rapid uptrend (Figure 196).

Figure 197 demonstrates another example of selecting priority cluster for USD/SEK.

Figure 197. Two clusters of resistance, USD/SEK, Daily

Figure 198. Construction of extension-II and selection of priority cluster, USD/SEK, Daily

Two clusters of resistance defined with retracement and projection could be used for USD/SEK sales (Figure 198). As regards the properties of levels, the upper cluster was stronger, as both were key levels. However, extension-II built on the last trend segment (X:A) indicated that the FE 100% + 50% cluster would be a priority for trading, as it fell into the buffer zone between the levels 127.2% and 161.8%. Figure 199 shows that after reaching a priority cluster, the USD/SEK pair dropped significantly.

Figure 199. Downturn in the price from priority resistance cluster, USD/SEK, Daily

The final example of selecting priority cluster is shown in Figures 200-203.

Figure 200. Two clusters of support, USD/CHF, H1

Figure 200 shows two clusters of support, USD/CHF, identified with retracement and extension of the first type. Given the fact that IP2 (38.2% - 14.6%) pattern is present in correction, the terminal cluster to be reached would be 61.8% + 161.8%. When building projection on the last trend segment of the, the upper top cluster 50% + 127.2% falls into the buffer zone (Figure 201).

Figure 201 Priority cluster of support, USD/CHF, H1

Figure 202. Formation of IP3 pattern, USD/CHF, H1

Figure 202 shows that the upper cluster of support fell into the buffer zone, so we can open a transaction to buy at the target level of 23.6% before the price reaches the lower cluster. When the price hits this level, IP3 pattern is formed, with the target cluster 61.8% + 161.8%.

Figure 203 demonstrates that the price started upward as soon as it hit the priority cluster, and reached the 23.6% level. This justified opening transactions for sale with the target level of 61.8%. Figure 203 shows that the USD/CHF pair hit the target cluster of support, which was initially located beyond the buffer zone.

Figure 203. Reaching the target cluster of support, USD/CHF, H1

Applying Extension-II to determine the priority cluster aids in identifying the area of support that can be used for transactions. When IPs are not formed in correction, Extension-II indicates the cluster of possible end of the correction. Otherwise, it indicates the cluster that can act as a component of some internal pattern of retracement. In this case, the trader receives more opportunities to trade within the price correction.

8.5. IP1 and IP2 on a cluster

Probable price reversal on a strong cluster of support or resistance is an indisputable fact. But how to use this knowledge in trading? Should we open a transaction from each cluster upon expectation of the price reversal from the selected area?

It's easy to guess that not every cluster will perform equally well. In some situations, the price can fail to stop on the cluster, and, thus hits the stop-loss.

To avoid chaotic trading based on composite clusters and random profits, I recommend using additional signals to determine, whether the price would rise or fall from a certain cluster.

The Comprehensive Fibonacci analysis uses only three additional signals, which allow entering the market from the cluster, with confidence that the price takes the right direction.

The first additional signal, formation of IP1 or IP2 on a cluster, is discussed in this chapter.

Figure 204. Composite support cluster, USD/JPY, Daily

Figure 205. IP1 pattern on the support cluster, USD/JPY, Daily

Figure 204 shows a support cluster on the USD/JPY currency pair. As soon as the price hits the cluster, the trader can enter into a transaction to buy; however, the more correct decision is to wait for an additional signal, such as IP1 or IP2 pattern on the support cluster. This pattern can be formed either on the timeframe of the defined support cluster (Daily timeframe in Figure 204), or "minor" timeframe (e.g., H4 is minor to daily timeframe). Figure 205 shows that the price formed IP1 pattern on the support cluster, H4 timeframe.

Is the emergence of IP1 or IP2 pattern on the cluster advantageous? Yes, greatly!

First, the pattern suggests that the price has a good chance to start rising or falling from the defined cluster of support. In such situation, trading is based on a cluster, whereas IP represents an additional signal to enter the market.

Second, the cluster as such does not indicate where to place take-profit and stop-loss orders after entering the market. We can define it only indirectly. In case, when IP1 or IP2 appears on a cluster, we can easily place orders, in line with the rules.

Figure 35 shows that buying USD/JPY was carried out on the basis of IP1 pattern formed on the cluster. Stop-loss order was placed below the 0% level and take-profit order was placed at 50%, according to the pattern rules.

Development of this situation is shown in Figure 206.

Figure 206. Reaching the target level IP1, USD/JPY, H4

The next example of IP formation on the cluster is shown in Figures 207-209.

Figure 207. Composite resistance clusters, USD/CHF, H4

Figure 208. IP1 pattern on the resistance cluster; retracement is built by points X:A; USD/CHF, H4

Figure 207 demonstrates resistance clusters defined with Fibonacci projection and extension-I. These clusters refer to H4 timeframe. After some time, IP1 pattern appeared on the same timeframe (Figure 208). To sell the USD/CHF pair relying on resistance clusters only would be risky, because a strong upward trend was observed at the moment. The emergence of IP1 pattern on clusters alerted us in advance that correction would develop up to the target 50% level. Figure 209 shows that the 50% level was hit after some time. Thus, IP1 on the cluster performed fine.

Figure 209. Reaching IP1 target level, USD/CHF, H4

Another example of IP formation on the support cluster is shown in Figures 210-213.

Figure 210. Composite support cluster, GBP/USD, Daily

Figure 210 demonstrates the support cluster on GBP/USD pair defined with projection and extension of type II. Buying an asset from the cluster, against a persistent downtrend, would be very risky. We must wait for an additional signal, such as IP1 or IP2 pattern on the cluster.

Figure 211. Formation of IP1 pattern on the cluster, GBP/USD, H4

Figure 212. Formation of IP2 pattern on the cluster, GBP/USD, H4

Figures 211 and 212 show that two patterns, IP1 and IP2, were formed in turn on the support cluster. The target levels shifted in the course of pattern formation. Arrows indicate the points of market entry, in line with IP1 and IP2 pattern rules. The outcome of this situation is shown in Figure 213.

Figure 213 Reaching the target cluster on the GBP/USD pair, H4

Was it possible to buy the GBP/USD pair, once it reached the composite support cluster? I believe, yes. However, such purchases would be made "blindly", since the trader is unaware, where the price can go and where to place stop-loss and take-profit orders. IP1 and IP2 models provide this information, and if these patterns emerge on the cluster, the trader must enter the market, as all the necessary conditions for trading are met.

And what about the simple clusters? Are IP1 and IP2 patterns formed on simple clusters, the same as on composite ones? Yes, of course! Let's take a look at Figures 214-216.

Figure 214. Simple key cluster of resistance, USD/CHF, Daily

Figure 215. IP1 pattern on a simple cluster of resistance, USD/CHF, H4

Figure 214 shows an already familiar situation on the USD/CHF pair. The resistance cluster was determined with retracement built on the trend of H4 timeframe and auxiliary retracement built after deep correction.

The price formed IP1 pattern on a minor timeframe (Figure 215) defined by building retracement by points X:A (a short-term hourly trend). Development of this situation is shown in Figure 216.

Figure 216. Reaching the target IP1 level, USD/CHF, H4

A few days after formation of IP1 on the cluster, the price started downward movement and eventually reached the target 50% level but did not hit the stop-loss order.

Composite clusters of support/resistance are called "the backbone of trading" for a good reason, as they are very important in the Comprehensive Fibonacci analysis. A properly defined cluster allows the trader to find the level where the price would reverse upon arrival. The trader must take advantage of the extremum formation and the subsequent price reversal, and make profit by opening a transaction in the direction of the price reversal.

The situation when IP1 or IP2 patterns are formed on the cluster increases odds of successful transaction and the trader receives hot information about the level of market entry and where to place take-profit and stop- loss orders.

In this chapter, we reviewed one of the three additional signals that are formed on clusters. Then we will discuss two other tools, no less important, which enable the search for a good entry point into the market.

Chapter 9
TOC pattern and its application under CFA

In addition to IP1 and IP2 patterns, a support/resistance cluster can form another great model; I have long and successfully used it in trading to complement the Comprehensive Fibonacci analysis.

This pattern enables opening transactions on clusters in the absence of IP1 or IP2; it also provides an excellent confirmation for opening a transaction at Level 2, in the internal retracement patterns.

To discover this pattern, we need to introduce an additional indicator – Price Channel[22] – (period = 20, shift = 2). As is known, the upper and lower borders of this indicator do not represent levels of support/resistance, but the price behavior at one of the channel borders is of great interest.

When a reversal pattern ("turn on the channel", TOC) is formed on the upper or lower border of the channel, make sure that the pattern is formed either on a support/resistance cluster, or at Level 2 of internal retracement pattern and then open a transaction.

This pattern makes a good confirmation to enter the market. Take profit and stop-loss orders are placed according to Fibonacci, whereas the emergence of TOC pattern is an important signal indicating that the price will go in the expected direction.

This pattern can emerge on any timeframe, but similarly to the Fibonacci tools, it can be used in trading on timeframes ranging from H1 to Monthly.

9.1. Formation of TOC pattern

Let's take a look at Figure 217, which shows forming TOC pattern on EUR/USD.

---

22. Also known as Donchian Channel

Figure 217. TOC pattern, EUR/USD, H1

When "turn on the channel" pattern is being formed, the following conditions should be met:

1. The price must break the upper or lower border of the channel (point 1, Figure 217). A breakout means anchoring either a full candle body or its larger part (2/3 or more), above or below the channel. If only the candle shadow went outside the channel, the situation is not considered as a breakout.

2. Then the price must return into the channel moving to the opposite border (point 2, Figure 217). At the same time, the opposite border must not be reached. Return of the price into the channel must be clearly visible.

3. The price must approach the previously broken border of the channel and form a signal candle. The candle shadow must be located outside the channel and the closing price for this candle must remain within the channel (point 3, Figure 217).

When all conditions are formed – we have TOC pattern, or the reversal pattern. Figure 217 shows a bearish version of TOC pattern. Let's see how the price behaved next (Figure 218).

Figure 218. Downward price reversal after TOC formation, EUR/USD, H1

Figure 218 shows that after forming "turn on the channel" pattern on the EUR/ USD pair, the price changed its direction from upward to downward and dropped by more than 50 points in a few hours.

Apart from the basic conditions for pattern formation, there is another important factor of timing, as the pattern must be formed within timeframe limits. The interval between the breakout of the upper/lower border of the channel (the first condition) and formation of the signal candle (the third condition) must not exceed:

- H1 – not more than 1 day
- H4 – not more than 1 week
- D – not more than 1 month
- W – not more than six months

For example, if TOC pattern appears on the H4 timeframe, the interval between the breakout/breakdown of the channel and formation of the signal candle should not exceed one week. If time limits are broken and the period of pattern formation went beyond the established terms, this pattern should not be used in trading. The same ban refers to the pattern, where the opposite border of the channel was reached during pattern formation (the second condition).

Let's review the following example of TOC formation.

Figure 219. TOC pattern on GBP/USD, H4

Figure 220. Implementation of TOC pattern, GBP/USD, H4

Figures 219 and 220 show the formation and implementation of bullish TOC pattern on the GBP/USD currency pair. Point 1 refers to the breakout of the lower channel border, after which the price returns into the channel and moves to the opposite border without reaching it (point 2). After that we observe the price drop to the lower channel border and formation of a signal candle, with its shadow below the channel border and the closing price within the channel. A transaction to buy must be opened upon formation of this candle and Figure 220 demonstrates that immediately after formation of TOC pattern the price started upward and increased by about 140 points from the entry point.

The signal candle, which triggers opening transaction on TOC pattern, can take a slightly different form than described previously. Quite often, the signal candle after forming the first and the second pattern conditions penetrates the channel border, thus, disrupting the rules of pattern formation. In such situations, we should consider the next emerging candle.

Figures 221 and 222 show such situation.

Figure 221. A special case of TOC pattern (bullish model), USD/CHF, H4

Figure 222. Implementation of TOC pattern, USD/CHF, H4

Figure 221 shows an example of TOC pattern, where the first and the second conditions are fulfilled completely and the third condition failed (no signal candle to be closed within the channel). In Figure 222, the lower channel border was broken by the candle, which was intended as a signal candle.

Naturally, in this case the transaction to buy is not opened, as the third condition is not met. In such situations, we should wait and consider another candle, which would form next to the failed signal candle, because:

- *If the candle that follows a failed signal candle is closed within the channel, we get the TOC pattern.*

In this case, we build upon the rule of superimposition, which is used in the analysis of candlestick patterns. If we superimpose visually a white candle onto the "signal" one (Figure 221), which broke the channel, we obtain a combined candle with a long lower shadow that meets the third condition of TOC pattern formation. Therefore, here we must consider both candles that form the third condition, and, accordingly, such situation can be regarded as an ordinary TOC pattern with a slightly modified signal candle.

Figures 223 and 224 present another example of TOC pattern with a special case of the signal candle.

Figure 223. TOC pattern, GBP/USD, H1

Figure 223 shows that the signal candle was closed on the upper channel border, after formation of the first two conditions, which is inconsistent with the rules of forming traditional TOC (closing price must be placed within the channel, rather than on its border). In this situation, we should wait for the next candle and Figure 223 shows that the next candle was "bearish" and, most importantly, it was closed within the channel. So, we have a common TOC pattern and, upon its completion, a transaction to sell GBP/USD should be opened.

Figure 224 shows the implementation of TOC pattern on GBP/USD.

Figure 224. Implementation of TOC pattern, GBP/USD, H1

This pattern resembles the "Turtle soup"[23] and "Turtle Soup Plus One" [24] models described by Linda Raschke in her book "Street Smarts". However, the rules of TOC formation are more specific and conditions of its emerging differ from the well-known patterns of Linda Raschke. For example, the first condition of pattern formation implies that the price must break the upper or lower border of the channel: formation of a new maximum or minimum (high or low) only is insufficient.

Let's take a look at the other examples of TOC pattern formation.

Figure 225. TOC patterns on USD/JPY, H1

Figure 225 demonstrates two TOC patterns formed on the USD/JPY currency pair. The first pattern was formed after the price falling and indicated its possible rise, which indeed followed in the future. After forming the bullish TOC, the currency pair gained 130 points. Later, another TOC pattern was formed on the USD/JPY, this time – the bearish pattern. The downtrend that followed was not long but the price dropped by 40 points. This made a good profit for intraday trading.

23. Linda Bradford Raschke, Laurence A. Connors, «Street Smarts: High Probability Short-Term Trading Strategies», M. Gordon Publishing Group, 1996, p.12

24.. ib., p.22

Figure 226. TOC pattern on GBP/JPY, H4

In Figure 226, the pattern is defined on the GBP/JPY currency pair. The model was formed after a long downtrend and GBP/JPY went upward immediately after formation of the signal candle. In 2 weeks, the currency pair gained 480 points.

Figure 227. TOC pattern on GBP/USD, Weekly

In Figure 227, the long-term TOC pattern is presented on the GBP/USD currency pair. This pattern persisted long enough and every condition of its formation was met: the price did not reach the opposite channel border and the interval between the breakout of the channel and formation of the signal candle made five and a half months, which is less than specified by the rules (six months). This pattern was a sign of long-term rise in the GBP/USD pair, which proceeds until present.

In fact, TOC pattern is a model that reveals traders, who prefer following the trend instead of seeking price reversals. This comes particularly well in the periods of flat market. In case of strong upward or downward trend, TOC pattern, upon its intrinsic feature as the reversal pattern, can send false signals. When this pattern is used in trading as a standalone model, the trader needs a "filter" to select suitable patterns with a high probability of profit. This would inevitably impose restrictions on trading capacity of this pattern.

As noted earlier, in Comprehensive Fibonacci analysis, TOC pattern is an auxiliary component; therefore Fibonacci traders don't need a filter. When we define the level of possible reversal (and, probably, time reversal?), we just need to wait for the emergence of TOC pattern and open a transaction if it appears. Given the high efficiency of the pattern and the Fibonacci tools, we expect to profit from this transaction.

TOC pattern presents the greatest interest to CFA when it is formed either on the cluster, or as part of IP pattern.

9.2. TOC on a cluster of support/resistance

As we already know from the previous chapter, one of the options for cluster-based trading is to open transactions upon IP1 or IP2 patterns that often emerge in the support/resistance areas. In situations, when IP pattern is not formed, the cluster can still be used in trading. Another common situation is opening transactions upon TOC formation on the cluster.

As in the case of internal retracement patterns, to open a transaction from the cluster using TOC pattern, we should move to the next lower timeframe. The pattern can be formed as well on a working timeframe with the cluster, but more often TOC appears on a minor timeframe, and this fact is sufficient for opening a transaction from the cluster, upon the available TOC.

Let's consider the first example of forming TOC pattern on the support cluster.

Figure 228. Patterns of support, EUR/USD, H4

Figure 228 highlights two clusters of support for EUR/USD: FE 150% + 38.2% and 61.8% + FE 200%. Both refer to the key clusters and while the second cluster consists of two key support levels, the most important cluster was determined with extension-II (Figure 229).

Figure 229. Identification of key clusters with extension-II, EUR/USD, H4

In the above chart, we see that the second support cluster fell into the buffer zone between the levels 127.2% and 161.8%. Therefore, it was selected for trading.

This situation offered several scenarios. Since entering into purchase from the cluster was risky (despite the strong enough cluster in this case), we could wait for: formation of TOC or IP on the minor timeframe, or formation of TOC on the working timeframe (H4). Here the first formed pattern (the earliest) on EUR/USD was TOC on H1 (Figure 230).

Figure 230. TOC on the support cluster, EUR/USD

A special case of TOC pattern was formed on the support cluster selected with extension-II. A transaction to buy must be opened upon formation of the signal bullish candle. We did not observe IP during correction, up to the moment when the price reached 50%, so, the first target of the purchase was placed at the level of 23.6%, as the level of possible IP3 formation.

Figure 231. The price reaches the 23.6% level, EUR/USD, H1

Figure 231 shows that the price gained easily 180 points and went up to the 23.6% level. No pattern for opening a transaction to sell was formed at this level; therefore, entry into the EUR/USD market was skipped.

In this situation, TOC pattern confirmed the "intention" of the price to reverse on the support cluster, which triggered the EUR/USD purchase.

Another example of TOC pattern on the cluster is demonstrated below.

Figure 232. Cluster support, USD/JPY, H4

The currency pair formed IP1 pattern and reached the key support cluster at the 50% level of retracement (Figure 232). So, as IP was formed, correction can be considered complete. To open a transaction, we must receive a confirmation, either in the form of TOC, or IP on the minor timeframe (H1).

Figure 233. TOC on the support cluster, USD/JPY, H1

TOC pattern was formed on the support cluster (Figure 233), slightly below but within its area, as seen on H4 timeframe. This cluster-based TOC triggered the opening of the USD/JPY purchases. The purpose of these purchases is quite obvious: to buy profitably an asset from the point of end of correction, from the lowest low. Figure 234 shows development of this situation.

Figure 234. Upturn in the price after TOC formation, USD/JPY, H1

Immediately after forming TOC pattern, the price went upward and increased by 160 points in three days. It presented a great opportunity to make money through buying USD/JPY at the lowest low, upon the TOC pattern formed on the support cluster.

Figure 235. TOC pattern on the support cluster, EUR/USD, H4

Figure 235 shows formation of TOC pattern on the EUR/USD currency pair. The cluster is defined by retracement and extension-I and consists of 50% + 127.2% levels. Here, the cluster refers to H4 timeframe where TOC pattern was formed. We have a support cluster and we have a pattern to open purchases. After entering the market, the price went upward and almost approached the 0% level; thus, the EUR/USD increased by more than 150 points (Figure 236).

Figure 236. Upturn in the EUR/USD pair from the support cluster + TOC

Figure 237. Resistance cluster on the NZD/USD currency pair, Daily

Figure 237 shows how the NZD /USD pair reached the resistance cluster defined with projection and extension-I. The cluster consists of FE 200% and 127.2% levels. This is an excellent level to enter into sales, but we must ensure that the price would not descend from this cluster. Later, the price formed TOC pattern on H4 timeframe, which made a confirmation for the sale entry (Figure 238).

Figure 238. TOC on the resistance cluster, NZD/USD, H4

Figure 239. Downturn in the price from the resistance cluster + TOC, NZD/USD, H4

Figure 239 shows that after formation of TOC on the resistance cluster, which appeared on the minor timeframe (H4 for Daily), the EUR/USD currency pair immediately went downward and dropped by 130 points in 3 days.

A final example of combined application of TOC and clusters is shown in Figures 240-242.

Figure 240. Resistance cluster on USD/SEK, Daily

Figure 241. TOC on the resistance cluster, USD/SEK, Daily

Figure 240 and 241 show that the USD/SEK currency pair, while forming upward correction, has reached the key resistance cluster 38.2% + FE 161.8%. Here the TOC pattern was formed (Figure 241), which triggered the USD/SEK sales. An interested reader will also notice another TOC on the FE 100% + 23.6% cluster, after which the price went downward, reached the 9% level and formed IP1 pattern.

Once the TOC pattern was formed on the 38.2% + FE 161.8 cluster, the price started falling and dropped by 100 points from the entry point, reaching the level of 14.6% and forming IP2 concurrently (Figure 242).

Figure 242. Downturn in the price from the resistance cluster after forming TOC, NZD/USD, Daily

Thus, we reviewed a few examples of forming TOC patterns on clusters. As noted previously, TOC pattern is often formed in the markets, but it is most important when appears at the key levels of support/resistance, which include the cluster.

Since the cluster alone cannot indicate, to what level the price can raise or drop, the target level should be defined either by the internal patterns of retracement or indirect signs. A good target for rise or drop of the price from the cluster can make another cluster located along the price path. In this situation, TOC pattern can be formed in both areas, which provides more chances for successful trading.

9.3. TOC + IP

Another trading option can be used when TOC pattern is formed within IP. Generally, this situation is implemented in FOREX through four options:

1. *TOC pattern is formed at Level 2.*
2. *TOC pattern is formed before the emergence of IP on the market highest high/ lowest low (maximum/minimum).*
3. *TOC pattern is formed at Level 1.*
4. *TOC pattern is formed at Target level.*

The options, where TOC pattern is formed within the IP, are listed below in descending order (by significance) and have the following properties:

- TOC formation at Level 2 is the most important condition for opening a transaction. In this situation, additional confirmation for the entry is not required
- IP formation follows formation of TOC pattern. It is a common situation, more often on Daily and H4 timeframes. Here, IP makes a confirmation to open transactions upon TOC. Additional confirmation to open a transaction is not required.
- TOC formation at Level 1 within IP is a rare case. In this situation, we must make sure that a cluster of support/resistance exists at Level 1; it is of no importance, whether it is a key or non-key cluster.
- TOC formation at «Target» level within IP requires the presence of a cluster at the same level. In its absence, TOC pattern must not be used in trading.

Relying on my long trading experience with CFA, I can conclude that forming TOC pattern at Level 2 within IP is the most significant situation, as only a small proportion of transactions ended with losses after the entry from TOC at Level 2. Other situations of TOC formation within IP can also be used in trading. The examples below demonstrate these options based on the availability of internal retracement pattern.

The first example of TOC formation at Level 1 is shown in Figure 243.

Figure 243. TOC pattern at Level 2, USD/JPY, H1

Figure 243 demonstrates formation of TOC pattern at the 9% level. IP2 pattern was preceded by the extended flat zone, where the price reached 38.2% and 14.6% levels. The 14.6% level failed to confirm the entry, due to the absence of resistance cluster on the currency pair. A few hours later, TOC pattern appeared at 9% and a transaction to sell was opened, in line with IP2 rules (Figure 244).

Figure 244. Reaching the target 61.8% level, USD/JPY, H1

Another example of TOC formation at Level 2 is shown in Figures 245 and 246.

Figure 245. TOC pattern at Level 2, USD/SEK, H4

Figure 246. Reaching the target 50% level, USD/SEK, H4

Figure 245 demonstrates that after a long downturn in the USD/SEK currency pair, IP1 pattern was formed within correction. TOC pattern was formed on the 9% level and thus provided a reason to buy the USD/SEK with stop-loss at 0% and the target at 50% level. Figure 246 shows that the target was reached in a short time.

Under some market situations, TOC appears both at Level 2 and Level 1. TOC pattern at Level 1 requires confirmation in the form of any resistance cluster. If confirmed, we can open a transaction at Level 2 as the target level. Figures 247-249 illustrate this situation.

Figure 247. TOC pattern at Level 1, USD/JPY, H1

Figure 248. TOC pattern at Level 2, USD/JPY, H1

Figure 248 shows that TOC pattern was formed at the 23.6% level. By applying Fibonacci projection to this level, we detected a cluster of resistance and, upon formation of the TOC signal candle, a transaction to sell was opened with the target at 9%. After reaching this level, the price formed another TOC pattern, which was confirmed by IP1. This provided a reason to buy USD/JPY at the target 50% level, upon the confirmed entry into the market. Figure 249 shows that the price reached the target IP1 level easily.

Figure 249. Reaching the target 50% level, USD/JPY, H1

Another common situation is the emergence of TOC before IP formation. In this case, TOC can be formed on the cluster and a transaction can be opened without additional confirmation.

But even if TOC is formed outside the cluster, it is still tradable. This is the case when TOC formation was followed by IP pattern (any pattern, not necessarily IP1 or IP2). The combination of TOC + IP provides a sufficient condition for entry into the market. At the same time, IP can appear either on the working timeframe, or on the minor timeframe (the next lower-order). Both options can be used in trading. Here we build upon the opposite: IP confirms TOC and not vice versa.

Figures 250-252 demonstrate examples of IP formation after the emergence of TOC.

Figure 250. TOC pattern, EUR/USD, H4

Figure 251. IP1 pattern, EUR/USD, H4

Figure 252. Reaching the target 50% level, EUR/USD, H1

Figures 251-252 show how IP1 pattern was formed after the emergence of TOC pattern on the EUR/USD; here, the internal retracement pattern acted as a confirmation for purchases of this currency pair.

TOC formation on H4 (Figure 250) and the subsequent emergence of IP1 on the minor timeframe H1 (Figure 251) triggered opening a transaction to buy, which soon brought nearly 140 points of profit. In this case, the presence of clusters was not required, because adequate conditions for purchase were formed by TOC + IP1.

Another example of TOC formation on IP is shown in Figures 253-257.

Figure 253. TOC on USD/CHF, Daily

Figure 254. IP3 pattern emerged after TOC formation, USD/CHF, Daily

Figure 253 shows that after the downturn of the USD/CHF currency pair, tradable TOC pattern appeared on the daily timeframe. As no significant clusters were observed in the lowest low, we needed to wait and make sure that the price can really implement this pattern. Figure 254 shows that the price went upward after TOC pattern was formed and, shortly, IP3 pattern emerged on the USD/CHF; thus confirming TOC pattern. A purchase with the target 61.8% level should be opened upon this pattern and the available proper conditions, TOC+IP3.

Figure 255. Additional TOC within IP3, USD/CHF, H4

Figure 256. The price reaches the target 61.8% level, USD/CHF, H4

Figure 255 shows that after entering the market upon IP3 from 23.6% level, the price dropped slightly and another TOC pattern was formed on the minor timeframe H4. This pattern confirmed once again that technical analysis of the higher Daily timeframe was conducted correctly and the price movement to 61.8% level could be expected. This really happened later: the target 61.8% level was reached through the price rally (Figure 256). Transactional profit from Level 2 amounted to 165 points.

Figure 256 also shows that reaching the 61.8% level coincided with the formation of TOC pattern on H4 timeframe. To enter into a transaction to sell upon this TOC, we must ensure that a strong enough cluster exists at the 61.8% level and it is capable to reverse the price.

Figure 257. Downturn in the price after reaching the target 61.8% level, USD/CHF, H4

The resistance cluster was identified with projection built by points X:A:B and extension-I built by points A:B (Figure 257). The cluster was indeed found at 61.8% level and TOC pattern could be used for opening a transaction to sell. Later, the USD/CHF price attempted to proceed upward, but was anchored by the resistance cluster and soon resumed the downtrend and almost approached the 0% level. This drop on the USD/CHF currency pair was predicted by TOC + resistance cluster.

Chapter 10.

Fibonacci time projection as a tool for analyzing "time" levels

Trading on the foreign exchange market with tools provided by the Comprehensive Fibonacci analysis represents a systemic and highly effective working method. Determination of the price level, where the extremum is formed, and the following price reversal combined with the TOC pattern, allows for wide trading opportunities on various currency pairs.

When developing the basic CFA rules and models, I have conducted research on numerous books dealing with this area of analysis. In some publications, I came across information about the tools indicating support/resistance price levels and even those indicative of time levels. These tools are called "Fibonacci time tools" and they are used to define a specific time point when the market trend changes its direction.

Upon studying the methods for constructing "time tools", as described in various books and trading guides, I concluded that there exist uniform plans for building time tools that ensure precise construction and, therefore, truly amazing results can be obtained by applying Fibo levels of time tools.

Such tool – Fibonacci Time projection – is used in the Comprehensive Fibonacci analysis. Time projection is constructed on clearly described patterns and by using this tool the CFA trader can determine the time moment when the market forms a particular price extremum.

It may seem surprising, but practical applications of time projection and examples presented in this Chapter suggest definitely that Fibonacci time projection can indicate the time of price reversal. Thus, the previously studied support/resistance tools would tell us "where" an extremum, or a pattern, would be formed in the market and Fibonacci time projection would tell "when" it happens.

The methods of construction and application of Fibonacci time projection presented in this Chapter are unique and the efficient analysis leaves no doubt about the applicability of this CFA tool.

10.1. Construction and application of time projection

To build Fibonacci time projection correctly, we must first define the pattern forming at the end of the upward or downward price movement. This pattern is called "two highs" or "two lows" and it occurs in the foreign exchange market very often. As a rule, this pattern is formed at the end of the upward or downward trend, regardless of its length (i.e., regardless of the analyzed timeframe); a pattern can be formed at the end of price correction, as well.

A schematic plan for constructing Fibonacci time projection is presented in Figures 258 and 259.

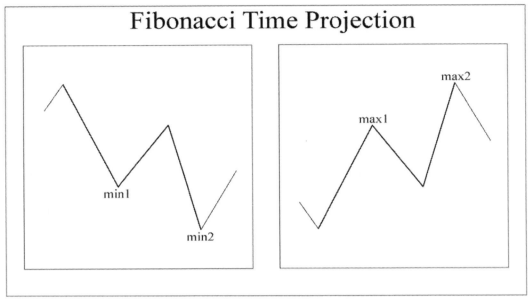

Figure 258. Schematic plan for constructing time projection on "two highs" and "two lows" patterns

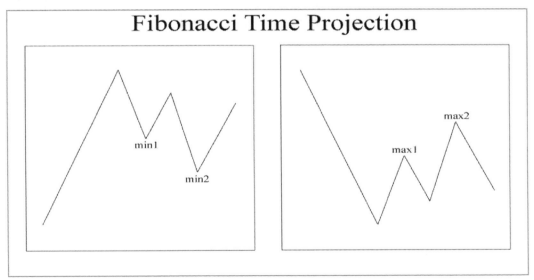

Figure 259. Schematic plan for constructing time projection on patterns formed at the end of correction.

The above schematic plans demonstrate clearly the principle of building time projection. To build the tool, we must find "two highs" or "two lows" patterns, and time projection is constructed between the extremes of the pattern. The extreme points should be selected very precisely, since their misplacement by even one bar/ one candle would induce an error in the analysis. While a small error is admissible in building retracement or projection, time projection should be built exactly on the bars, which made maxima/minima (highs/lows) for the price movement.

The following levels are used in the Fibonacci time projection tool:

- T 0%
- T 100%
- T 161.8%
- T 200%
- T 261.8%
- T 300%

All levels included in this list are equal in terms of their "strength". Levels T 0% and T 100% are used for building the tool and are not included in the analysis. T 300% is the last time level and when the price passes it, time projection should be rebuilt.

With view of systemic use of time projections in the analysis and trading, a simple rule is followed: if an upward price trend was observed before the level of time projection, the price will change direction after passing this level. Conversely, the downtrend observed prior to reaching Fibonacci time level can stop after hitting this level and the market will start rising.

With this in mind, the optimal trading moment is the situation when the price approaches time projection level directionally, i.e., it clearly rises or falls. To determine, whether the price would further rise or fall in case of flat price is very difficult before the time projection level is reached. In such situations, we should consider the entire price movement that occurred prior to the moment when the price approaches the level of Fibonacci time projection.

Figure 260. "Two highs" pattern, EUR/GBP, Daily

Figure 260 demonstrates the "two highs" pattern formed on the EUR/GBP daily chart. The days that should be included in building Fibonacci time projection are marked as max1 and max2. Figure 261 shows construction of the tool upon the selected pattern.

Figure 261. Fibonacci time projection, EUR/GBP, Daily

Time projection built on the "two highs" pattern has worked perfectly: after passing each Fibonacci level on the EUR/USD currency pair, the price formed an extremum and then reversed.

As the price went beyond the T 300% level, time projection should be rebuilt. The currency pair continued its downward movement and hence, we should proceed with the "two highs" pattern. Figure 261 shows that a good extremum suitable for building the tool appeared to the left of max1. If we take this maximum, time projection can be extended to cover the current price changes on EUR/GBP (Figure 262).

Figure 262. Fibonacci time projection, EUR/GBP, Daily

When rebuilding time projection on the long-term "two highs" pattern, the T 161.8% level gets included into historical price movement and thus, cannot be used in the analysis. However, we still have three time levels, where the price would form the extremes and possibly change the direction of movement. Figure 263 shows development of this situation.

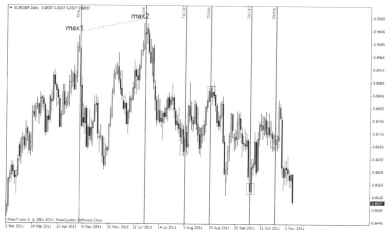

Figure 263. Price movement at the levels of Fibonacci time projection, EUR/GBP, Daily

Turn attention to Figure 263. The price move changed its direction after passing the levels T 200%, T 261.8% and T 300%. If the price moved downward prior to reaching the time projection level, it started upward after hitting the level, and vice versa.

One can think that such price behavior at time projection levels is a coincidence, but numerous trade situations and market examples confirm that it is not in the least accidental: Fibonacci time projection actually points to the time moment, when the market can form an extremum and the subsequent price reversal. The examples below illustrate this statement in detail.

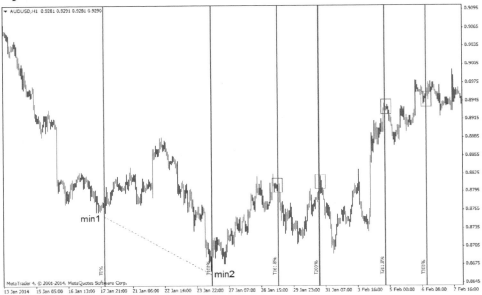

Figure 264. Fibonacci time projection, AUD/USD, H1

As is the case with other CFA tools, time projection can be applied unrestrictedly on various timeframes, from H1 to Monthly. Moreover, this tool performs equally well on different price segments, both long- and short-term. However, very short patterns are unsuitable for constructing time projection, because Fibo levels of this tool would be located too close to each other and thus complicate the analysis.

Figure 264 demonstrates construction of Fibonacci time projection on AUD/ USD. As can be seen, all levels of the tool performed accurately and indicated the time moments of forming price extremes. The best performance is observed at levels T 161.8%, T 200% and T 261.8%: the price was rising until hitting these levels and started falling after that. T 300% level performed well, too, but indicated a short reversal area – here the price formed a local extremum.

Figure 265. Fibonacci time projection, EUR/USD-H4

Figure 265 shows an example of constructing real-time Fibonacci time projection used in the EUR/USD trading. It can be noticed that the price reversed after passing each time level: downward movement was reversed to upward at the T 161.8% level and upward movement – to downward, at T 200% and T 261.8% levels. The current price approaches the T 300% level and its future trend is determined by the direction of approach.

In Figure 265, max1 and max2 points build time projection. Another extremum is observed between these points, but this one is not to be used for the analysis, because the levels of time projection on this maximum are placed densely and this prevents from evaluating the long-term price changes.

Figures 266-268 present a few more examples of Fibonacci time projection.

Figure 266. Fibonacci time projection, USD/CAD, Daily

Figure 266 shows an example of time projection on USD/CAD. As is seen from the chart, the price changed direction after passing each time projection level. The best performance was demonstrated at levels T 161.8% and T 300%. Importantly, in case of T 261.8% level, the earlier price movement was directed upward, but the trend disappeared when approaching this level and IP was formed at the minor timeframe. In view of the prior upward trend, a sharp drop in the price after hitting T 261.8% level looks quite logical.

Figure 267. Fibonacci time projection, EUR/USD Daily

In Figure 267, time projection is built on a long-term "two highs" pattern. Points max1 and max2 were particularly prominent in the chart and the tool was built through these extremes. When the price hit the Fibonacci levels, we observed a change in its direction. T 161.8% indicated the local extremum, after which the price started its uptrend. T 200% level indicated perfectly the day of reversal, after which the upward price movement on the EUR/USD pair was completed and a rapid decline was set.

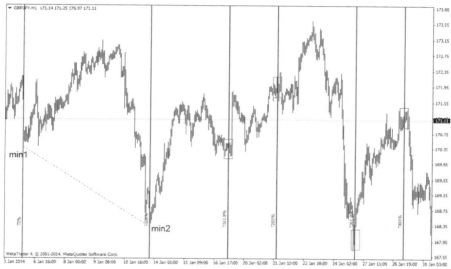

Figure 268. Fibonacci time projection, GBP/JPY, H1

Turn attention to Figure 268. This example allows us to trace the price movement around time projection levels and reinforce our understanding of how to apply this tool. Penetrating each level of Fibonacci time projection was accompanied by the change of price direction, as follows: the upward price trend before – hitting the level – the downward price trend after, and vice versa.

Getting such excellent level properties in Fibonacci time projections is quite easy. All you need is to correctly build a tool on "two lows" or "two highs" pattern, upon selecting the proper extremes.

10.2. Specifics of constructing the tool

The above-discussed construction of Fibonacci time projection on a pattern is a unique method and, as is seen from examples, this tool makes the price follow the Fibonacci levels like a wizard. Now, when building correct Fibonacci time projection on the highs and lows, we can define time zones, where the price will change its direction from upward to downward, or vice versa. And this feature should be necessarily used in trading!

Since time projection is built on the Fibonacci pattern and lots of patterns emerge on the FOREX, in some situations, we can build even two tools rather than one. In such cases, the first time projection is built on the "two highs" pattern and the second time projection – on the "two lows" pattern. Independent levels of both time projections are used in the analysis; moreover, the overlapping levels produced by these two tools are also important and can be used for trading. These are cases of "time" clusters, i.e., the areas, where levels of different time projections are placed very close.

Let's take a look at Figures 269 and 270.

Figure 269. Two time projections, USD/JPY, H1

Figure 270. Price reversal on a "time" cluster, USD/JPY, H1

Figure 269 demonstrates construction of two time projections on the USD/JPY currency pair. The first time projection is built on the "two lows" pattern (points min1 and min2) and the second - on the" two highs" pattern (points max1 and max2). Both time projections indicated a time cluster, which was observed on the USD/JPY chart. The pair dropped up to the "time" cluster and therefore, after penetrating the cluster we could expect change of direction, which did occur, in fact (Figure 270).

Figures 271 and 272 exemplify clustered construction of time projection.

Figure 271. Two time projections, AUD/USD, H1

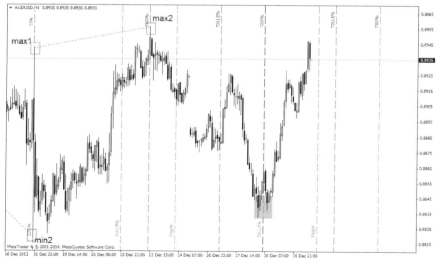

Figure 272. Price reversal on a "time" cluster, AUD/USD, H1

In Figures 271 and 272, time projections are built on the AUD/USD currency pair. Two patterns were selected for construction: "two highs" and "two lows". Further, we defined "time" cluster consisting of two levels of time projection, T 200% and T 261.8%. The AUD/USD pair declined up to the "time" cluster and the price reversed subsequently.

The final example of clustered construction of time projection is shown in Figures 273 and 274.

Figure 273. Two Fibonacci time projections, EUR/USD-H4

Figure 274. Price reversal on a "time" cluster, EUR/USD, H4

Examples of clustered construction (time projections, Figures 273 and 274) demonstrate the price behavior at individual levels and provide the evaluation of "time" cluster as a set of levels. Here, the cluster consists of levels T 161.8% and T 200%. The EUR/USD pair went uptrend, up to the "time" cluster and started downtrend immediately after penetrating the area of accumulated time levels.

Considering these examples, we can conclude that if paired construction of time projection is feasible (both "two highs" and "two lows" patterns are present in the chart), the so-called "time" clusters – aggregations of time levels from different tools – come to be very important for analysis and trading. These aggregation zones act as strong reversals, and opening transactions orders from areas of clustered time levels allows the trader to capture the moment of reversal for a specific currency pair.

10.3. "Place" + "time" in the CFA

Against the undeniable advantages of Fibonacci time projection to trading, we should mention the fact that with this tool alone we cannot decide on the strength of the price reversal after penetrating the "time" level. In most situations, Fibonacci time projection can indicate the moment of extremum formation but it is difficult to evaluate, how long the subsequent price reversal will be. It can be either a short-term price correction, or a fundamental change in the direction of price movement.

As noted earlier, Fibonacci time projection is an auxiliary tool and successful trading needs application of other basic Fibo tools, as well, such as retracement, extension, and projection. When a trader applies Fibonacci tools comprehensively, he can determine both the level of price reversal, and the time, when this reversal starts. In this case, the entry point should be selected with consideration of Fibonacci time projection and the take-profit and stop-loss orders should be set with key Fibonacci tools.

Situations when the price and time levels coincide in a certain area of the chart are rather frequent in the FOREX market. Here, time projection can be indicative of:

• Support/resistance cluster,
• IP1 pattern (on one of the key pattern levels),
• TOC pattern

In such situations, the trader clearly understands both "where" to open a transaction and "when" it should be opened. The Comprehensive Fibonacci analysis provides complete information about the future price changes.

Let us review examples of complex application of Fibonacci tools, when the market coincided in "place" and "time".

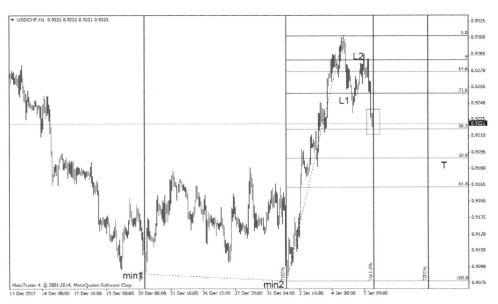

Figure 275. Fibonacci retracement + Fibonacci time projection, USD/CHF, H1

Figure 276. Support cluster, USD/CHF, H1

Figure 275 demonstrates an example of building Fibonacci retracement and time projection on the USD/CHF pair. After the start of downward correction, the price formed IP1 pattern targeted at the 50% level. The support cluster was defined by projection at the 38.2% level (Figure 276) and, as is seen in the chart, the T 161.8 % level of Fibonacci time projection also indicates this support cluster. Since the price moved downward before reaching this cluster, the upward movement could be expected after penetrating the T 161.8% level.

Figure 277. IP2 pattern + T 200% level, USD/CHF, H1

Figure 278. IP2 pattern on the auxiliary retracement, USD/CHF, H1

Figure 277 shows that after reaching the support cluster and penetrating the T 161.8% level, the price movement reversed its direction, from downward to upward. During the upward move, the price formed IP2 pattern and, thus, its correction was supported by two IPs. Reaching the 14.6% level and IP2 formation coincided with reaching the T 200% time level. As the former price trend was directed upward, we could expect its reversal to downward, as soon as the price penetrated this level.

To make sure of the further price drop, we build the auxiliary retracement on the L1:L2 segment of IP2 pattern. Figure 278 shows that the internal IP2 pattern was formed on the auxiliary retracement. This confirmed the speculation about the further price drop, which occurred soon afterwards (Figure 279).

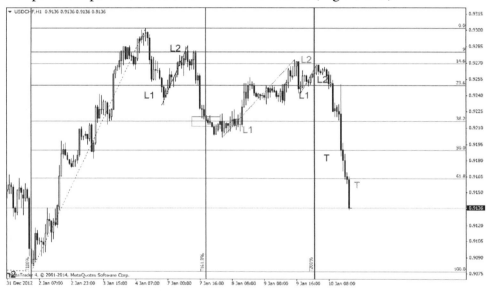

Figure 279. Reaching the IP1 and IP2 target levels, USD/CHF, H1

Immediately after passing the T 200% time level, the price started downward and ultimately both target levels, IP 50% and 61.8%, were reached. Time projection performed well twice: T 161.8% level indicated the price reversal from the 38.2% level and T 200% indicated the possibility of implementing IP2 pattern (including the internal IP2 pattern).

The following example demonstrates the comprehensive analysis for the EUR/USD pair, at the moment of formation IP3 price pattern.

Figure 280. Fibonacci time projection + IP3, EUR/USD-H4

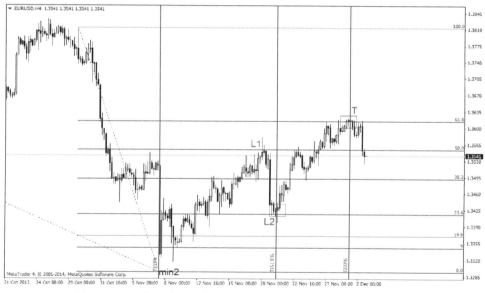

Figure 281. Reaching the 61.8% target level, EUR/USD/H4

Figure 280 demonstrates an example of the EUR/USD comprehensive analysis performed with retracement and time projection. In the process of forming IP3 pattern, the price approached the first time level - T 161.8% under a downward trend and after penetrating this level, the reversal and upward price movement can be expected. This is also confirmed by the formed IP3 pattern targeted at 61.8%.

In the future, the price reached 61.8% level (Figure 281) and T 200% Fibonacci time projection was also observed at this level. As can be seen from the chart, by reaching the 61.8% level, the pair formed a downward correction: since the EUR/USD pair demonstrated an uptrend before the T 200% level, after penetrating the time level, its downtrend could be predicted.

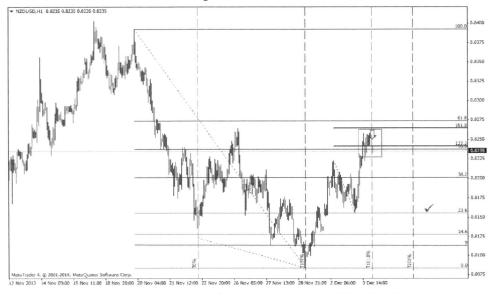

Figure 282. Resistance cluster + T 161.8%, NZD/USD, H1

Figure 283. IP3 pattern + T 200%, NZD/USD, H1

Another example of complex interaction between "place" and "time" levels is shown in Figure 282. Here, the price correction reached the cluster at the level of 50%, as defined with Fibonacci I-extension. This cluster was indicated by T 161.8% and the previous uptrend was expected to change by the downtrend after reaching this time level. In view of the possible IP3 formation, the situation required placing a stop-loss order beyond the 61.8% level and the take-profit order – at the 23.6% level.

Figure 283 shows that the price dropped starting from 50% and reached the 23.6% level. The candle on the H1 timeframe that reached 23.6%, fell on the time level T 200%! Price drop up to the T 200% level and the presence of IP3 pattern suggest that a transaction on the pattern should be opened, where T 200% acts as an auxiliary element predicting the price uptrend. Development of this situation is shown in Figure 284. As is seen in the chart, the 61.8% target level was easily reached by the price.

Figure 284. Reaching the 61.8% target level, NZD/USD, H1

Other examples of application of Fibonacci time projection are shown in Figures 285-288. Here, the time level indicated not only the support cluster, but also TOC pattern, which confirmed the possibility of the ended correction on the USD/CAD currency pair.

Figure 285. Support cluster + T 161.8%, USD/CAD

Figure 286. TOC pattern + T 161.8%

Figures 285 and 286 show the place of decision-making to enter the USD/CAD purchase: support cluster + T 161.8% time level. During correction process, the price failed to form an IP (both 38.2% and 9% levels were not reached) and reached 61.8%, where the composite key support cluster was identified with the help of FE 138.2% projection level (key level for USD/CAD).

The presence of Fibonacci time projection level within such cluster makes an adequate prerequisite for entering the market (in our case, a purchase). However, this condition is not informative as to whether this would be a slight increase, or the price would follow the trend by refreshing the 0% level. For verification, we need either the IP on a minor timeframe, or the available TOC pattern. Figure 286 demonstrates that TOC pattern emerged in the area of Fibonacci time level and it suggests that in case of purchases, the USD/CAD target should be above 0%, because the correction could be complete. Figure 287 shows further price changes in USD/CAD.

Figure 287. The price uptrend from TOC pattern on a cluster + T 161.8%

The final helpful example is demonstrated in Figure 288. Here, the projection time level is built on the USD/JPY currency pair.

Figure 288. Fibonacci time projection + TOC patterns, USD/JPY, H1

TOC pattern is an excellent model to capture both short- and long-term price reversals. In the latter case, the pattern must be formed at the support/resistance level/cluster.

If TOC pattern is formed at the level of Fibonacci time projection, this makes an appropriate condition for opening a transaction. An important factor to be considered is matching timeframes of the time pattern and TOC projection: they should refer to the same timeframe. Figure 288 exemplifies the alternate formation of two TOC patterns on the T 161.8% and T 200% levels. Levels of the time projection indicated the region of pattern formation, instead of the signal candle, but this is quite sufficient for opening a transaction upon this TOC.

In this situation, all we need is determining the point of the market exit, which can be done simply with the help of Fibonacci retracement, projection, or extension. These tools were discussed in detail in the relevant chapters.

Chapter 11

Examples of applying comprehensive Fibonacci analysis in FOREX trading

While working on this book, various trading situations emerged in the FOREX market, which gave rise to opening numerous transactions. In these situations, the entry decision was taken both with "place" and "time" tools, as well as upon the internal retracement patterns and the TOC pattern. Nine diverse trading situations were selected and are reviewed in this chapter. Rules of construction and applications of Fibonacci tools were discussed earlier. Here we consider trading examples based on the Comprehensive Fibonacci analysis.

11.1. AUD/USD: IP2

Due to the reduced price from the II-extension, IP2 pattern was formed (Figure 289). In addition, the AUD/USD pair reached the 50% retracement level of the weekly trend and this confirmed a possible price reversal according to IP2 pattern.

Figure 289. IP2 pattern on AUD/USD, H4

After opening the purchase transaction at the 14.6% level, the price did not move upwards immediately. For some time, the AUD/USD fluctuated between the levels of 38.2% and 14.6%. Against this flat, it was decided to open an additional purchase of a smaller volume, since the price level was still appropriate. The cumulative profit from two purchases was expected to be greater than that of one pair purchase (Figure 290).

Figure 290. Additional purchase of AUD/USD, H4

Figure 290 demonstrates that the stop-loss order for the second purchase was placed below the 9% level. The expectation implied that the price would soon start moving to the target level, without persisting the flat. Setting stop-loss on the second purchase at the 0% level, like in the first case, was not quite profitable, as the entry level was disadvantageous. The outcome of this situation is shown in Figure 291.

Figure 291. Reaching the 61.8% level for AUD/USD, H4

The above figure demonstrates that the target level of 61.8% was ultimately reached in IP2 pattern. Two purchases opened upon IP pattern brought 188+146 points.

In this situation, AUD/USD buying was opened on the basis of IP2 pattern, which was confirmed by a strong 50% support level, which was reached by this pair on January 24, 2014.

11.2. GBP/USD: TOC + IP1

After a prolonged decline, the GBP/USD pair established a TOC pattern (Figure 292). This pattern was formed on the cluster, though not strong enough to justify the immediate purchase of GBP/USD. A confirmation for this TOC should be awaited.

Figure 292. TOC on GBP/USD, H4

IP1 pattern emerged as a confirmation of the previously formed TOC on GBP/USD. This pattern was formed on the hourly downtrend, and made a starting point for trading the pair (Figure 293). The established IP1 indicated the 50% target level, as well as the stop-loss level. However, taking into account the TOC pattern and the presence of support cluster, the stop-loss order was placed below the support cluster, instead of placing it below the 0% level.

Figure 293. IP1 pattern on GBP/USD, H1

Following the IP1 pattern formation, the GBP/USD pair started upward and the price has reached eventually the 50% level (Figure 294). In this situation, the transaction was opened in line with the trend and, therefore, buying could be proceeded further on. The level of purchases acted as an additional positive factor: a transaction on the GBP/USD purchase was opened at a local minimum.

Figure 294. Reaching the 50% level on GBP/USD, H1

GBP/USD purchases brought a profit of 114 points. Buying was triggered by the TOC pattern on H4 timeframe and IP1 pattern, as a confirmation to the market entry.

11.3. USD/SEK: IP3 + resistance cluster

Figure 295 demonstrates an example of another transaction made on the basis of Comprehensive Fibonacci analysis. In this example for the USD/SEK pair, a reason to sell appeared in the form of IP3 pattern on the H1 timeframe.

Figure 295. IP3 pattern on USD/SEK, H1

The above figure demonstrates a visible IP3 pattern, which was formed upon the IP1pattern. In this case we have a set of patterns: IP1 reached the 50% target level, whereas the price move, from 50% to 23.6%, refers to IP3 pattern.

To confirm the possible price decline within IP3, we used a resistance cluster derived from the built Fibonacci projection. This cluster is a non-key and contains two levels – 23.6% and FE 61.8%. According to the property of the 61.8% FE level, this cluster can prevent the rising trend of the price. With this in mind, a decision was taken to sell USD/SEK upon IP3, with the target at the 61.8% level. However, in this case we observed a target cluster, rather than a target level, since 61.8% was close to FE 200%. The transaction was scheduled to be closed upon reaching the cluster.

Figure 296. Development of IP3pattern, USD/SEK, H1

Figure 296 demonstrates that the price did not rise above the cluster 23.6% + FE 161.8%. It made a turning level for USD/SEK and after "touching" the cluster the pair started downward move.

Relying on the projection built, a large number of short-term support levels were observed on the plot including the previously reached cluster 50% + FE 161.8%. In this situation, it was decided to shift the stop-loss order to the breakeven zone, in order to hedge against the possible growth from strong supports.

The outcome of this situation is shown in Figure 297.

Figure 297. Reaching the USD/SEK target cluster, H1

As seen in Figure 297, the price has not yet started the rise but continued its technical move within the IP3 pattern. Its decline went until reaching the key support cluster and the transaction to sell was closed upon touching this cluster. The profit from this transaction made +50 points.

USD/SEK sales were opened on the basis of IP3 pattern and the resistance cluster 23.6% + FE 61.8%.

11.4. EUR/GBP: FE100% + IP2

Another example of transaction made with the retracement and projection is shown in Figure 298. IP2 pattern was formed on EUR/GBP and indicated a possible decrease of the currency pair.

Figure 298. IP2 pattern on EUR/GBP, H1

Figure 298 demonstrates a Fibonacci projection on the large first and second waves for the EUR/GBP pair. Considering the properties of FE 100%, it acted as a strong resistance level in this situation. At this level, the «three little Indians» pattern was formed and IP2 emerged after the price reversal. Since the 14.6% level coincided with the FE 100% level, it was decided to enter the sale on this pair. Orders were placed upon the IP2 pattern rules. In Figure 298 we can also observe a key support cluster formed by 50% + FE 61.8% levels. It could suspend the price; therefore, it was decided to fix most of profit at this cluster and to hold the remainder until reaching the 61.8% level.

Figure 299 demonstrates development of this situation.

Figure 299. Reaching the 61.8% target level, EUR/GBP, H1

As seen in Figure 299, the price did not change pace at the support cluster 50% + FE 61.8%. Following the publication of fundamental statistics, the EUR/GBP pair dropped sharply, broke the support cluster, and immediately reached the 61.8% target level, where the take-profit order was set.

The profit from this decline within IP2 made 67 points. The EUR/GBP sell was opened upon IP2 pattern + strong resistance level FE 100%.

11.5. EUR/USD: 50% + T161.8%

An example of applying time tools to trading is shown in Figure 300. Here, in the process of upward correction the EUR/USD pair reached the "place + time" area, which made the starting point for sales.

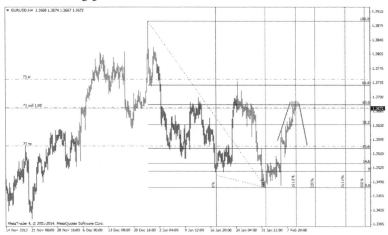

Figure 300. "Place + time" on EUR/USD, H4

The place where the EUR/USD sale started is indicated in Figure 300. The entry was made on the basis of 50% retracement level and T161.8% level. Since no other entry confirmations were established, the transaction was opened with a small lot. The 61.8% level was selected as the place for setting the stop-loss order, whereas the 23.6% level was selected as the target level (similar to the IP3 pattern). Orders could be set more precisely if the confirmation appears on the junior timeframe. Figure 301 demonstrates development of this situation.

Figure 301. Point of inversion (downtrend) for the EUR/USD pair, H4

As seen from the above figure, the price began to decline immediately after reaching the 50% level. Or reckoning was quite obvious: if the price showed an upward trend, up to the T161.8% level, then it might reverse upon hitting this level, which happened actually for the EUR/USD pair. Along with that, an additional pattern emerged shortly on the H1 timeframe, which indicated the possibility of further decline (Figure 302).

Figure 302. IP1 pattern for EUR/USD, H1

During the downward progression of the price (from the 50% level), IP1 pattern appeared on the hourly EUR/USD chart – an excellent confirmation to proceed with sales. With view of this pattern, the primary target was selected properly: the 23.6% level coincided with the 50% short-term retracement level. Thus, a simple key cluster acted as a target level for the EUR/USD decline. Upon the formation of IP1pattern, the stop-loss order was shifted to the break-even zone.

Figure 303 demonstrates the outcome of these sales for the EUR/USD pair.

Figure 303. Reaching the target cluster, EUR/USD, H1

The target cluster at the 50% level was hit simply through one candlestick! A sharp drop occurred after the IP1 formation, but this pattern was only auxiliary to the root causes of opening the transaction – the 50% "place" level and T 161.8% "time" level. The profit from this transaction made 96 points.

11.6. GBP/CAD: T261.8% + IP1

In the above sample transactions based on Comprehensive Fibonacci analysis, I built upon patterns and clusters when opening purchase and sale transactions. In the case of GBP/CAD currency pair, a transaction was opened upon the Fibonacci time projection, whereas retracement patterns acted as supplements.

Figure 304 demonstrates that the price approached the T261.8% level. This time level indicated the possibility of reversal. Before hitting this level, the price dropped within a downward correction and, therefore, one would expect an upward trend afterwards.

This Fibonacci time projection was built upon two candlesticks: min1 – August 16, 2012, and min2 - March 12, 2013. Figure 304 demonstrates that the first-level tool, T161.8%, performed rather implicitly, whereas the T200% level indicated clearly a day of reversal followed by GBP/CAD correction. Then the GBP/CAD pair approached the T261.8% level (Figure 304) and IP1 pattern was formed on the H1 timeframe, as a confirmation of purchase (Figure 305).

Figure 304. T261.8% level, GBP/CAD, Daily

Figure 305. IP1pattern, GBP/CAD, H1

IP1 pattern on the H1 timeframe was identified with delay and at the moment of opening the transaction, upon the T261.8% level and IP1 pattern, the entry was placed far above the 9% level (Figure 305). The distance from the stop-loss level to the take-profit level was almost the same, which was not the best. Though, the chances of earning were high against the upward expectations in the price, after penetration the T261.8% level.

In this case, the key resistance cluster 61.8% + FE 200% made a more attractive target, rather than the 50% level, including the expectation of continued upward trend.

Figure 306 demonstrates the subsequent price behavior.

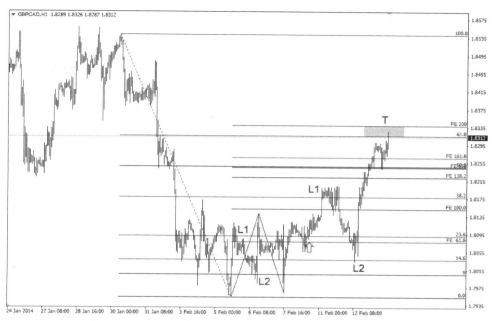

Figure 306. Reaching the target cluster, GBP/CAD, H1

After entering the market for the GBP/CAD pair, the price started moving upward, but was restrained further by the 38.2% level. Finally, another pattern (IP2) was formed for the currency pair. Since the first transaction entry was not particularly successful, I decided against opening yet another purchase transaction but, according to the IP trading rules, the second model should be used for additional purchases, to increase the cumulative profit.

After some time, the price reached the target resistance cluster and this transaction made a profit of 200 points. Reaching the T261.8% level and IP1 pattern, as a confirmation to enter the market, opened the transaction.

11.7. USD/SEK: TOC + IP2

In the next example, the transaction was opened on the USD/SEK currency pair. After the formation of short-term downtrend on the H1 timeframe, the TOC pattern was established (Figure 307). In terms of clusters/support levels, the TOC pattern appeared "from nothing", with no support clusters to explain the downtrend, or the key Fibonacci levels to justify the USD/SEK purchase. In this situation, the only proper solution was waiting for the possible formation of additional pattern (since IPs could be formed on the USD/SEK through the TOC) and open the transaction upon the available additional pattern. Figure 307 demonstrates that IP2 pattern appeared after the formation of the TOC on USD/SEK.

Figure 307. TOC pattern + IP2, USD/SEK, H1

Opening the transaction on the basis of the TOC only is incorrect, because in this case we have no information about the levels of setting take-profit and stop-loss orders needed for systemic trading. After the IP2 pattern appears, we face the standard situation when the internal pattern confirms the possibility of price reversal and at the same time we know, where to place either a stop-loss or a take-profit order.

Let's examine it further.

Figure 308. Reaching the 50% target level, USD/SEK, H1

Figure 308 demonstrates that after a 2-day flat period, the currency pair revived and reached the target level of profit at the 61.8 % level, in an hour. The profit on this transaction made 50 points.

11.8. EUR/USD: IP4 + IP3

Sets of patterns in the foreign exchange market represent a good trading option, since the profit can originate from several IPs, instead of a single-source profit. However, it is not always the case that all patterns of the set bring profit.

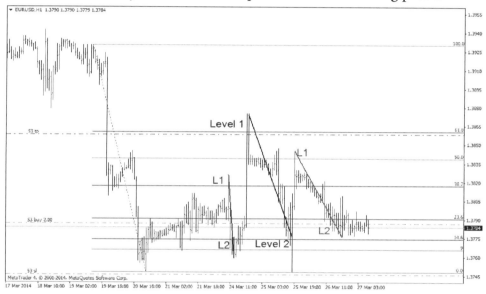

Figure 309. IP2 + IP4 + IP3, EUR/USD, H1

Figure 309 demonstrates a sample transaction opened upon the IP4 + IP3 set. Prior to that, IP2 pattern was formed on the time trend (hourly) retracement and the price reached the 61.8% target level. Further, in line with all pattern rules, two IPs were formed on the EUR/USD: the fourth and the third models. The target and the stop-loss levels in these models were identical. This is a very rare set in the foreign exchange market and I had great expectations of IP4 and IP3. IP2 model made a profit and, if other patterns succeeded in shifting the price up to the 61.8% level, the situation would have been just perfect. However, something went wrong.

Figure 310. Reaching the stop-loss level, EUR/USD, H1

Figure 310 demonstrates that instead of reaching the 61.8% level, the downward trend persisted and the price reached the breakdown level – cancelled scenario by a stop-loss order. The total purchase of 2 lots opened upon the IP4+IP2 set, ended with a loss.

Were these losses avoidable? I believe, yes. When we deal with a set of patterns, we are always faced a difficult task – to evaluate the probability of firing in models that follow the first one. In the case of EUR/USD (Figure 309), we see IP2 pattern that reaches the 61.8% level and in this situation correction on the currency pair should be considered complete, since IP is already formed and the key retracement level is reached.

To increase the chances of implementing the patterns, we use clusters, the TOC pattern, and temporal Fibonacci tools. In this situation, a purchase based on the set was made without confirmation because H1 – the "fast" timeframe and the corresponding confirmation had no time to be formed.

With regard to the trading outcomes in this correction for the EUR/USD pair, it should be noted that the profit from IP2 superseded losses on purchases from IP4 + IP3. This is explained by a high profit/loss ratio, which is characteristic of the internal patterns of retracement (undoubtedly, a positive feature).

11.9. GBP/USD: 61.8% + T261.8%

A few days ago, a transaction was opened on the GBP/US pair, which can be called an "ideal", fitting into all rules of the Comprehensive Fibonacci analysis.

Figure 311 demonstrates that after formation of IP2, as indicated by the T161.8% level, the pair reached the 61.8% level. Since IP2 pattern reached the target, correction in the currency pair is considered complete. In addition to reaching the target (61.8%), the temporal T261.8% level was also present in this area.

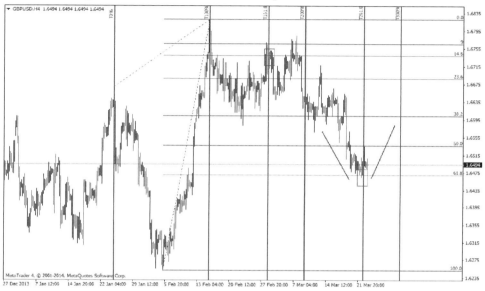

Figure 311. The 61.8% level and T261.8%, GBP/USD, H4

Figure 312. GBP/USD purchase and additional purchase, H1

Figure 312 demonstrates that the purchase was opened from the local minimum formed on GBP/USD. After that, IP1 pattern was formed on time (hourly) retracement, which established the target and the stop-loss level for this purchase. Considering its targets on the senior timeframe (for example, the opportunity to form IP4), the take-profit order was not fixed at the first stage.

When the price reached the 50% level and then decreased slightly, it was decided to open an additional purchase on the rising momentum from the EMA (21). This exponential moving average provides a great support to the price during the period of sharp growth and an excellent resistance throughout a sharp drop. Despite the fact that trading on a bounce from the EMA is rather an exception to the rule, it was justified in this situation.

After the second entry, the 61.8% target level was selected for both purchases. Development of this situation is shown in Figure 313.

Figure 313. Reaching the 61.8% target level, GBP/USD, H1

After entry on the purchase from the EMA (21), a sharp rise in the price followed and the GBP/USD pair easily reached the 61.8% level, where take-profit orders were set for both purchases. Two purchases on GBP/USD pair brought 132 + 46 points in profit.

Now let's examine the same chart in terms of support/resistance clusters (Figure 314).

Figure 314. Support/resistance clusters on GBP/USD, H1

Figure 314 demonstrates positioning of support/resistance clusters estimated by constructing a Fibonacci projection in addition to retracement.

It is clearly seen that as soon as the price increased, up to the key resistance cluster 50% + FE 161.8%, it formed an extremum and then declined. Decline in the price went up to the support cluster, which consists of 38.2% + FE 100% levels. At this level, an additional GBP/USD purchase was opened from the EMA, with the period of 21. From the point of view of Comprehensive Fibonacci analysis, a support cluster was observed there, which prevented further decline of the price.

11.10. Summary

To conclude this review on application of the Comprehensive Fibonacci analysis in trading, it should be noted that despite numerous tools used in the analysis, the majority of transactions are based on the same scenario. Most often, the market entry is made either from patterns (IP or TOC) formed upon the support or resistance, or the transaction is opened with "time" tools, which can indicate both the support/resistance cluster, and the formed IP or TOC patterns.

The above examples of transactions represent a small part of all opportunities provided for successful trading by the Comprehensive Fibonacci analysis in previous years and nowadays. Remembering that these unified rules of construction and trading tools are pioneer in the technical analysis, every reader of the book can apply this knowledge in practice. Despite the fact that the Comprehensive Fibonacci analysis should not be expressly referred to as a "trading system", trading with the CFA tools is systemic and meets all requirements of the modern technical analysis.

Conclusion

In summarizing our study of Comprehensive Fibonacci analysis, it should be noted that after reading this book, every trader and technical analyst, regardless of their professional experience, can apply unique Fibonacci methods in their operations. Possibly, some readers will prefer combining Fibonacci tools with supplementary analytic methods (indicators, candlestick patterns, etc.). As already mentioned in the book, the CFA represents an independent method for analysis and trading, which does not need extra confirmation. However, if the analyst takes an individual approach to apply the CFA, it proves to be far more productive, rather than to blindly follow the classical canons of technical analysis using Fibonacci tools. Moreover, if this tailored approach requires for a combination of the CFA with other analytical concepts – it does not contradict the principles of the Comprehensive Fibonacci analysis.

Development of Fibonacci tools, from classical methods to Comprehensive Fibonacci analysis, allows us to consider the entire Fibonacci analysis as a system, which evolves concurrently with the financial markets. This brings a great advantage to this type of technical analysis, meaning that it takes an up-to-date approach to trading in financial markets. The basics of technical analysis remain the same and do not require modifications, but the evolution of methods of analysis and trading is an inevitable process, beneficial to any technical tool to be used in everyday trading operations.

In conclusion, I again wish every success to my readers and colleagues. I will be happy to discuss with you any issues related to the Comprehensive Fibonacci analysis and in case you have any questions on possible cooperation, please do not hesitate to contact me directly.

To get the actual information about the CFA and to contact me, please visit: http://fibomaster.com/

Appendix. Just a few words about TOC pattern

TOC pattern is the only model in Comprehensive Fibonacci analysis defined with the indicator. The basis of the analysis and trading are the Fibonacci tools, whereas TOC pattern makes possible transactions when information received from the Fibonacci tools is insufficient.

The price can form TOC pattern anyplace in the market; however, its application to trading requires that the pattern emerged:

- on the cluster of support/ resistance
- at Level 2 within the IP
- before the IP formation
- at Level 1
- at Target level

In all the above situations, TOC pattern provides a great confirmation to enter the market. This pattern is actually needed in the Comprehensive Fibonacci analysis, because we can take advantage of the larger number of market situations. In cases of lack of information (when only IP or a cluster is available), TOC formation gives a great opportunity for opening transactions and meeting the expected price targets.

For example:

Figure I. TOC pattern on the support cluster, GBP/USD, H4

Figure I shows that TOC pattern was formed on the support cluster. This is a key cluster and it consists of FE 161.8 % + 61.8 % levels. Forming TOC pattern on the cluster provides a sufficient condition for buying GBP/USD. IP1 pattern was formed previously in correction and the price reached the key retracement level – so, we have complete correction. Take-profit order was placed beyond the 0% level and stop-loss order – beyond the lowest low of the signal candle of TOC pattern.

Figure II. Upturn in the EUR/USD after TOC formation, H4

The outcome of this transaction is shown in Figure II. After opening GBP/USD purchase in the volume of 3 lots, the market became strengthened and a sharp increase in prices in the next few days brought a profit of 110 points.

Bibliography

Hobbs D., «Fibonacci for the Active Trader», TradingMarkets Publishing Group. 2004

Carney S., «Harmonic Trading: Volume One», FT press, 2010

Gartley H.M., «Profits in the Stock Market», WA: Lambert-Gann, 1935

Pesavento L., «Fibonacci ratios with pattern recognition», Traders Press, 1997

Fischer R., «Fibonacci Applications and Strategies for Traders», Wiley, 1993

Fischer R., «The new Fibonacci Trader. Tools & Strategies for Trading Success», Wiley, 2001

Copsey I., «Harmonic Elliott Wave: The Case for Modification of R. N. Elliott's Impulsive Wave Structure», Wiley, 2011

Schwager J., «Schwager on Futures: Technical Analysis», Wiley, 1995

MacLean G., «Fibonacci and Gann Applications in Financial Markets», Wiley, 2005

Miner R., «Dynamic Trading, Traders Press», 2002

Boroden C., «Fibonacci Trading: How to Master the Time and Price Advantage», McGraw-Hill, 2008

Recommended Readings

- Warren Buffett Talks to MBA Students by Warren Buffett

- Stock Options: The Greatest Wealth Building Tool Ever Invented by Daniel Mollat

- You Can Still Make It In The Market by Nicolas Darvas

- Show Me Your Options! The Guide to Complete Confidence for Every Stock and Options Trader Seeking Consistent, Predictable Returns by Steve Burns, Christopher Ebert

- Invest like a Billionaire: If you are not watching the best investor in the world, who are you watching?

- Back to School: Question & Answer Session with Business Students by Warren Buffett

- New Trader, Rich Trader: How to Make Money in the Stock Market by Steve Burns

Available at www.bnpublishing.com

Made in the USA
Lexington, KY
16 May 2016